Business Rule Concepts

The New Mechanics of Business Information Systems

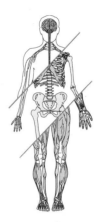

by Ronald G. Ross
Editor, *DataToKnowledge Newsletter*

Business Rule Solutions, Inc.
Gladys S.W. Lam, Publisher

Business Rule Concepts
The New Mechanics of Business Information Systems

Ronald G. Ross

10 9 8 7 6 5 4 3 2 1

ISBN 0-941049-04-3

To Vanessa

Acknowledgements

I would like to thank Keri Anderson Healy for her editorial assistance, and her many suggestions for clarifying and enhancing the content of this book.

I also wish to thank Gladys S.W. Lam and Mark Wilson for their long hours of toil on the lay-out of the book—and for their patience with me in the whole publication process.

Finally, I wish to thank Barbara von Halle for her support in making this book possible.

Contents

Chapter 4

Chapter 5

Appendix

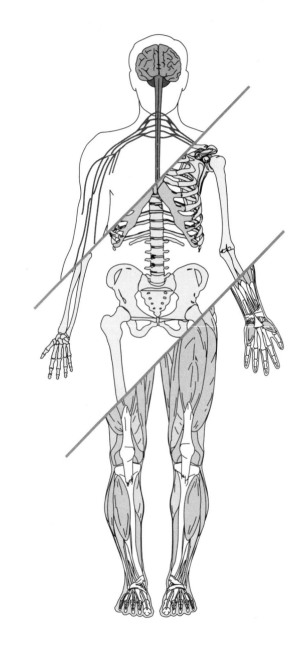

Introduction

The Business Rule Vision

The Marvelous Organism

The human body is marvelous in many respects, not the least of which is its mechanics. Roughly, support for the mechanics of the human body has three basic components, separate yet intimately interconnected, as follows.

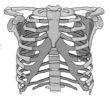

Structure: This is provided by the bones, which are organized and connected into the skeleton. The skeleton provides both a framework for carrying the weight of the other components, as well as a semi-rigid scheme around which the other "softer" components can be organized.

Power: This is provided through the muscles, which are connected to the bones. The muscles enable motion based on the framework provided by the skeleton. Since motion is what we see happening from outside the human body, the muscles seem most directly responsible for the behavior we perceive.

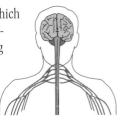

Control: This is provided by the nervous system, which connects to the muscles. Nerves connect muscle-to-muscle, through long series of connections passing through the brain. Response to all stimuli are coordinated through the firing of nerve impulses—no firing, no movement, and therefore no behavior.

These basic mechanical components are familiar to us all. In a moment, we will see how the mechanics of a business information system can be viewed in the very same terms. First, however, several observations about the mechanics of the human body are worth keeping in mind.

◆ First, all three components are essential. The human body literally cannot function without all three.

◆ Second, the three components are all interconnected—that is, integrated with each other. For example, tendons connect muscle to bone. Successful behavior depends on this integration.

◆ Third, the three components are specialized for a particular role or responsibility. Each optimizes for its particular task. Mixing or combining them would provide a less effective solution. Also, specialization provides for greater simplicity. Think about how much more complex bones would be if they incorporated muscles—or how much more complex muscles would be if they incorporated nerves.

◆ Fourth, the nervous system in some sense is the most important since it provides control for the others. The body is certainly capable of behavior without a well-organized nervous system—but not of effective, adaptive behavior. Literally, we cannot operate at our best with only half a brain!

We believe that business information systems should be similarly organized. Let's revisit the three components, thinking now of a business in place of a human body.

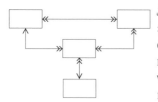 *Structure:* This is provided by the terms and facts,[1] which are organized and connected into a data model. The data model provides a framework, in many ways like a skeleton, in two basic respects.

◆ It carries the "weight" of the organization—that is, the eventual database it describes will carry the cumulative record of past interactions (*aka* history).

◆ It literally provides a semi-rigid scheme around which the other

---

1. Specifically, terms represent things of interest, and facts represent the logical connections between them. The exact analogy to the human body is therefore that terms represent the bones, and facts represent the ligaments—the bone-to-bone connections.

components can be organized—i.e., the basic ideas (*aka* semantics) common throughout the given business.

Power: This is provided by processes, which operate on the facts in the data model. Whereas the data model provides structure, the processes enable activity.

When we look at a business information system, the processes are often the most visible aspect because they literally "do" what the business needs to get done (e.g., take the customer's order). However, viewing a business information system as merely a collection of processes makes no more sense than viewing the human body as merely a collection of muscles. Any organism is much more than that—whether a human or a business.

Control: This is provided by rules, which constrain processes ("the muscles") to act only in certain ways deemed best for the business as a

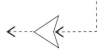

whole. In the human body, there are literally hundreds of muscles, which must act in concert. If they do not, the resulting behavior at best will be less than optimal. At worst, serious damage

can result (e.g., hyperextension of a limb) which will reduce the body's overall "behavioral" capacity substantially.

Similarly, a business and its information systems literally consist of hundreds (or thousands) of "muscles" (processes), which must act in concert. If they do not, the business will also "behave" in a less-than-optimal fashion. In some cases, serious damage can result (e.g., loss of customers, squandering of resources or opportunities, etc.), which will reduce the business' overall "behavioral" (i.e., competitive) capacity substantially.

We suggest that a business is very much like a human body—a living organism. Because of its complexity, we also suggest that its information systems should be organized in a corresponding manner.

Let's revisit the observations we made earlier about the mechanics of the human body, now applying them to business information systems.

◆ First, all three components—terms and facts (data model), processes, and rules—are essential. A business literally falls apart— disintegrates—without all of them.

◆ Second, the three components are obviously interconnected. For example, processes act to create, modify or delete instances of things represented in the data model. Effective integration is essential because successful business "behavior" depends on it. The point is that system development methodologies—or strategies for business process re-engineering (BPR)—cannot attack them in a completely segregated fashion and hope for an integrated result.

◆ Third, the three components are all specialized for a particular role or responsibility, each optimized for its particular task. Mixing or combining them would provide a less effective solution. With respect to business information systems, the importance of pursuing a data model "separately" from process modeling has been accepted by most professionals for many years. With the business rule approach comes recognition of the importance of also separating rules. We call this *Rule Independence*.[2] As a fringe benefit comes a huge simplification in the processes—the "muscles" of the business information system. In the business rule approach it is legitimate for the first time to talk of truly thin processes—a long-standing goal among IT professionals.

◆ Fourth, in some sense rules are the most important component since they provide control for the others. The business and its information systems are certainly capable of behavior without a well-organized set of rules—but not effective, adaptive behavior. Literally, rules are what makes a business more than "half smart" in how it operates.

Summary

The analogy to the human body points out that there are three basic components in understanding its mechanics:

◆ Structure (skeleton).

◆ Power (muscle).

◆ Control (nerves).

To comprehend fully how the human body works in a mechanical sense, understanding how these three components interact with one another is of paramount importance. However, each component also has its own inner workings—and indeed, there are individual sciences focusing almost exclusively on each

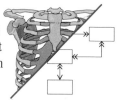

---

2. Ronald G. Ross, "The Declaration of Rule Independence," *DataToKnowledge Newsletter* (formerly *Data Base Newsletter*), Nov./Dec., 1995, p 24. (Reproduced in Appendix 1.)

particular component.

A business information system similarly has three basic components to its mechanics, as follows.

◆ Structure (terms and facts[3]).

◆ Power (processes).

◆ Control (rules).

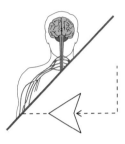

A complete understanding of the mechanics of an information system requires understanding how all three components interrelate in an integrated fashion. This, of course, represents the new vision that the business rule approach inspires. We believe its implications for businesses and business information systems is profound.

About this Book

Each of the three basic components in the business rule approach must be understood individually. Each has its own particular "physiology." These physiologies are examined in the remainder of this book.

This examination is divided into two parts. The first part explains the basic concepts of each component. It is aimed at the general reader who is seeking the basic message of the business rule approach. Although based in information system architecture, this part explores implications for the business and its use of information technology (IT). These implications culminate in Chapter 3, which presents revolutionary new ideas for organizing work for the information age.

The second part is aimed at the practitioner seeking deeper understanding of business rule concepts related to data models and rules.

Part I. The Message of the Business Rule Approach

◆ Chapter 1 examines structure, as embodied in terms and facts. This chapter provides the business rule view of data models and what they represent.

---

3. As provided by the data model.

◆ Chapter 2 examines control, as embodied in rules. This chapter provides exciting new insights about the inner workings of rules.

◆ Chapter 3 examines power, as embodied in processes. The business rule approach offers a new view of processes—one that is radical in its simplicity. Ironically, it is in that very simplicity that the "big picture" of information systems in the business rule approach emerges.

Part II. Business Rule Concepts for the Practitioner

◆ Chapter 4 re-examines structure, as embodied in terms and facts. This chapter explains the business rule approach to data modeling.

◆ Chapter 5 re-examines control, as embodied in rules. This chapter develops and explains fundamental rule concepts and categories.

Part I

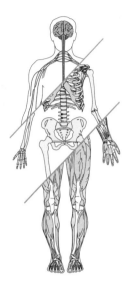

The Message of the Business Rule Approach

Chapter 1

What You Need to Know About Terms and Facts in the Business Rule Approach

In the human body, structure is provided by the bones, which are organized and connected into the skeleton. The skeleton provides both a framework for carrying the weight of the other components, as well as a semi-rigid scheme around which the other "softer" components can be organized.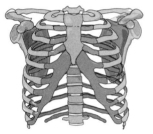

A business information system must have similar "structure." In the business rule approach, this structure is provided by a *data model*.

Many IT professionals think they already understand what data models are about. Unfortunately, they sometimes think of a data model as merely a technical design for a database. The business rule approach views a data model as much, much more—one *directly* connected with the business.

Not coincidentally, many non-IT workers and managers in the business sometimes are intimidated by data models. This is unfortunate, for two reasons.

◆ First, there is no need to view a data model as a technical design—at least not until late in the system development life cycle. There is no *need* to be intimidated by a data model for that reason. A good data model can be hard to create—but it should *not* be hard to understand.

◆ Second, these non-IT workers and managers are the ones with what it takes to *create* a good data model. It is what *they* know that makes all the difference in the world.

The business rule approach not only depends on "good" data models, but also offers a radically new perception of what they are about. Without any exaggeration, a good data model is no less important to a business information system than a strong and complete skeleton is to the human body.

The discussion that follows presents the new view of data models offered by the business rule approach. Chapter 4 explores the concepts of data models in greater detail, and indicates how data models should be developed for best results given a business rule approach.

The Business Rule View of Data Models

Ask managers and workers in the business what they mean by "requirements" for developing business information systems, and typically you get answers centered on functions to be performed, or the look-and-feel of how the system behaves through its interfaces (e.g., GUIs). "Data model" is not exactly always among the first responses.

Yet in the business rule approach, a data model represents the most fundamental type of "requirement" because it represents the basic component of what the company *knows*. Of course, it is by no means the *only* type of requirement, but it is one that must be addressed to provide real meaning ("sense") to the others.

> *Data models are a type of requirement.*

In the business rule approach, data models literally do just that—provide *meaning*. Unfortunately, this "meaning" is abstract—it is not as obvious as what a system does, or how it looks on the outside. But just because something is less obvious does not mean it is any less important—break a bone, and see what happens to a body's behavior!

> *Data models provide meaning.*

So if a data model is about defining requirements and meaning, why is it called a *data* model at all?[1] Why do we call the power of a car motor

---

1. The term "entity modeling" or entity-relationship (ER) modeling became popular as a replacement in the mid 1980s. However, these terms lost favor in the first part of the 1990s, along with the general dissatisfaction over first-generation CASE tools (for other reasons).

"horsepower?" ...where a plane takes off and lands a "runway?" ...where you store E-mail a "folder?" The reason is simply because we often try to make something new understandable by naming it after the old things it replaces. That is the case with respect to "data" model in the business rule approach.

Let's be clear about this. A data model can and should ultimately provide a blueprint for how *data* is physically organized in a database. However, this is the end result—a goal we work toward, There is *much* more to it than that. Consider another analogy.

When we pay an architect to create a blueprint, we expect a house that looks like the blueprint to come out of it eventually. Assuming that happens, then at that point, the blueprint reflects a reality—the house itself. But for the longest time (seemingly forever if you have been through it), the blueprint is nothing more than an organized attempt to determine our basic "requirements." It does not really describe the house itself—but what we *want* for the house. And to be perfectly frank, deciding what we *want* is often the hardest part of all. (That's why we have architects to help us!)

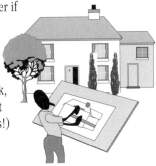

Terms and Facts

Returning to the human body, we see that the skeleton has two basic components—the bones and the ligaments, which connect the bones. Even though the bones are larger, and in a sense more basic, both are essential.

A data model represents the basic "skeleton" providing structure to a business information system. As in the skeleton for the human body, it likewise has two basic components, *terms* and *facts*. These are equivalent to the bones and ligaments, respectively, in the human body.

Terms. These are the basic words or terms that we recognize and share. These are simple or qualified nouns. Here are some examples.

customer	employee-name	date
prospect	delivery-date-due	high-risk customer
shipment	manager	employee
order	gender	line item
invoice	status	quantity-back-ordered

Facts. These are simple, declarative statements that relate the terms, much as ligaments connect bones in the human body. Here are some examples.

- Customer *places* order.
- Order *is included on* shipment.
- Employee *has* gender.
- Manager *is an* employee.

Note that in each of these cases, a *verb* or *verb phrase* connects terms previously listed. Since the terms exist apart from the facts, facts are usually identified with the verbs or verb phrases.

Several observations are worth making.

◆ First, terms and facts represent the common nouns and verbs of the business. (They also include common adjectives since some nouns are qualified, e.g., high-risk.) In other words, a data model is about establishing a common business vocabulary—one that we all agree to use in consistent fashion. In one sense a data model is as simple as that— it is the means we use to avoid a *Tower of Business Babel* in building complex information systems to conduct business. Here then is a fundamental principle of the business rule approach—*we will inevitably work more effectively if we all speak the same language.*

> In the business rule approach, a data model establishes common business vocabulary.

◆ Second, a data model represents *types* of things rather than instances of those things. For example, a business may have 10,000 customers, but these are represented by a single term, *customer*.[2] Similarly, customers may have placed 100,000 orders, but this connection is represented by a single fact, *customer places order*.[3] In general, the data model establishes the types of things we can "talk" about (i.e., share information about) within the business.

> A data model indicates the type of things we can talk about and share information about in the business.

◆ Third, every fact is *always* established using a complete sentence, following a strict subject-verb-object structure—for example, *customer places order*.[4] Such a sentence defines something that it is possible *to know* about.[5] The collection of *all* such sentences establishes the full and complete scope of the business information system in a very important sense. Even if a worker or some automated process produces some other facts, we will literally have no way to record or share instances of these facts unless the facts have been included in the data model.

> A data model establishes the basic scope of what the company knows.

---

2. Since the term refers to the type, rather than to instances, most data modeling techniques prescribe the singular form for nouns.

3. These 100,000 interactions represent *instances* of the fact, *customer places order*. If stored in a database, such instances (i.e., data) represent individual *facts*. *Customer places order* actually represents the fact *type* that organizes them. Since this discussion is not formal, we will use "fact" even when we mean "fact type."

4. In formal terms, such sentences represent *predicates*. *Every* business rule is a predicate.

5. That is, to *share*. Workers may know many things (i.e., types of facts). The data model establishes which of these facts they will *share*.

◆ Fourth, the sentences merely *establish* facts; they place *no* constraints on *instances* of these facts. For example, *customer places order* represents a fact. It is inappropriate to state the following as a fact per se. *Customer may place no more than 15 orders.* This latter statement is *more* than a fact—it places *constraints* on instances of the original fact. It is a rule—part of the

control aspect of the business information system, *not* part of the structural aspect. A rule represents *nerves*, not skeleton.

> Facts recognize what it is possible to know, but given that, no other constraints.

◆ Fifth, note how the facts are expressed using verbs (e.g., *places*). It is important to remember that these verbs do *not* represent an action or a process per se. They do not label some action or procedure (e.g., *place* order). Such an action represents a different aspect of the business information system—the power or "muscle" aspect. Think of the data model as providing an optimal structure[6] to record the *results* of such processes or actions. In other words, terms and facts organize what we can know *as the result* of actions or procedures taking place in the business.

> Data models organize the results of actions, not how the actions take place.

---

6. This means anomaly-free and semantically clear. In relational theory, normalization prescribes tests (the normal forms) to ensure this.

Using Graphic Data Models

The reader may have noticed that even though data models are usually rendered graphically, no diagrammatic examples have yet been presented. This is not because they are not useful—just the opposite is true; they are *very* useful. Rather, we wanted to emphasize that a data model is about what we can *know*. *"What we can know" can always be expressed in natural language sentences.*

Earlier, we made the point that data models represent a type of requirement—namely, terms and facts to be held in common. We want to emphasize that sponsors of business rule projects must sign off on the *sentences*—not on graphic data models. Most methodologies and CASE tools have this more or less *backwards!*

> The deliverable of the data modeling part of a business rule project is a set of declarative sentences.

Now it might seem that "writing sentences" will be a lot easier than creating data models. Are we letting everyone off easy? No! Sponsors and users must originate and understand the sentences—and business analysts and data modelers must help clarify and express them in plain business language (e.g., English). This is *hard*—not because English or any other natural language is hard, but because thinking how to express what we know about the business in understandable, agreed-to form is hard!

Even harder than this is getting all the sentences to fit together as if in some large jig-saw puzzle. This is where the graphic data model plays an important role.

In creating a blueprint for remodeling your house, you can quickly see when the pieces are not fitting together. The eye often spots it quite easily. A data model serves a similar purpose. In working with sentences, especially a large set representing a complex area of the business, it's often hard to spot redundancies and overlap. Representing them graphically makes this easier.

Figure 1 presents a simple data model in graphic form to illustrate. The facts from this data model are listed below.

Figure 1. Sample Data Model for a Library

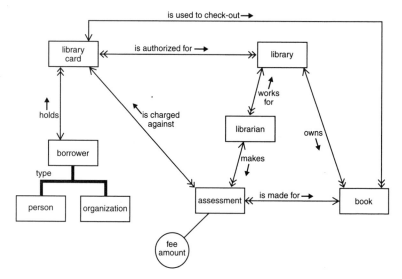

Library Facts:

◆ Borrower is a person or organization.

◆ Borrower holds library cards.

◆ Library card is authorized for certain libraries.

◆ Library owns books.

◆ Librarian works for a library.

◆ Library card is used to check-out books.

◆ Librarian makes assessments.

◆ Assessment is made for a book.

◆ Assessment is charged against a library card.

A good data modeler seeks to ensure that every fact is represented in the data model one and only one time, and does not overlap any other facts. In other words, the data model ensures that facts are *unified* and *unique*. Later on, this will provide a means to ensure that all rules are defined consistently, and that different actions will operate in consistent fashion.

> *By helping to ensure unification and uniqueness of facts, the data model ensures consistency in business behavior.*

Like the skeleton in the human body, the facts in a data model must represent the *minimum* set needed to provide a framework for the other

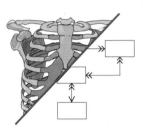

components. There are no "extra" bones in the human body—every one has a specific purpose. Adding a bone here or there is *not* going to improve on the body's mechanics. Anyway, bones are "expensive" because although essential, they represent "overhead" to the end result—which is behavior.

Similarly, a few "extra" facts here or there in the data model will not help the business body operate. And they will prove expensive. A data model helps ensure there are no "extra" facts for the business.

> *A data model should represent a minimum set of facts.*

Creating a minimum set of unified and unique facts in the data model is hard—but that is still *not* the hardest part. The *hardest* part is getting everyone to *agree* to this common "picture" of the business. This is often *very* challenging!

We find that IT professionals *consistently* underestimate the difficulty of creating good data models, and budgeting sufficient time for it. Some professionals believe that if they can get the behavior right, the structure will simply fall into place. That is not our experience at all! It's the body whole that matters. You can design a lot of very elegant appendages, and a lot of fancy behaviors, but there had better be a well-considered skeleton to hold them all together!

Chapter 2

What You Need to Know About Rules in the Business Rule Approach

In the human body, control is provided by the nervous system, an organized collection of nerves that connect to the muscles. Responses to all stimuli are coordinated through the firing of nerve impulses—no firing, no movement, and therefore no behavior.

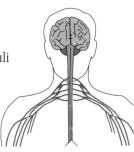

A business information system must have similar control over behavior. In the business rule approach, this control is provided by *rules*.

Rules for Control

Rules are familiar to all of us in real life—we play games by rules, we live under a legal system based on a set of rules, we set rules for our children, etc.

Yet the idea of rules in information systems is ironically foreign to most IT professionals. Say "rules" and many IT professionals think vaguely of expert systems or artificial intelligence—approaches deemed appropriate only for very specialized, often very advanced types of problems. There is little recognition of how central rules actually are to the basic, day-to-day operations of the business.

Not coincidentally, many non-IT workers and managers in the business have become so well indoctrinated in the *procedural* views of business activities that thinking in terms of rules may initially seem foreign and very abstract. Virtually every methodology is guilty in this regard—structured analysis, information engineering, object orientation, BPR, etc. This is unfortunate, for two reasons.

◆ First, thinking about the control aspect of any organized activity in terms of rules is actually very natural. For example, try imagining explaining any game—chess, checkers, baseball, football, tennis, etc.—without explaining the rules on which the "moves" in the game are based. Even if it were possible—that's doubtful—this certainly wouldn't be a very effective way to do it.

◆ Second, these non-IT workers and managers are the ones who have what it takes to *create* good rules. It is what *they* know that makes all the difference in the world in playing the "game."

The business rule approach not only depends on "good" rules, but also offers a radically new perception of what they are about. Without any exaggeration, good rules are no less important to a business information system than a robust, finely-tuned nervous system is to the human body.

The first step in understanding the central role of rules in the business rule approach is simply to relate them to the issue of control. In the special box opposite a light sampling of typical rules is presented, each categorized according to the type of control it addresses.

Note how far-ranging these categories of control really are. *Every* aspect of control in a business information system—or indeed of the business itself—can be addressed by rules. The reader should spend some time with these samples to fully appreciate the connection between rules and control. We will return to this important point later on.

> Rules provide control in the business rule approach.

Before we dig any deeper into using rules for control, however, we need to state several caveats. The subject of rules is a big one. There are several things this chapter does not attempt to do.

◆ First, it does not discuss how to capture rules, or to express them in

Sample Rules

Constraints
A customer must not place more than three rush orders charged to its credit account.

Heuristics
A customer with preferred status should have its orders filled immediately.

Computations
A customer's annual order volume must be computed as total sales closed during the company's fiscal year.

Inference
A customer that places more than five orders over $1,000 must be automatically considered "preferred."

Timing
A customer that places no orders for 36 consecutive months must be automatically archived.

some appropriate language.[1]

◆ Second, it does not explore detailed variations in rules, or provide a framework for categorizing them. Chapter 5 examines this area in greater detail.

◆ Third, even though this discussion and the follow-on discussion in Chapter 5 touch on important theoretical issues, these issues are not fully developed in this book. Our goal here is simply to explain rules—not develop formalisms.[2]

---

1. Business Rule Solutions, Inc. (BRS) publishes *Practitioner's Guides* and offers the BRS Business Rule Methodology to assist with these areas.

2. Refer to *The Business Rule Book* (Second Edition, 1997), by Ronald G. Ross, published by Business Rule Solutions, Inc.

Rules and Events

Automated information systems have addressed validation and editing of data since the first computer programs for business were written.

That is certainly nothing new. Unfortunately, the programmatic view of editing and validating data is a very procedural one—simply because traditional computer programs *work* that way. However, with respect to rules—that is, business rules—the procedural view is a very limiting one. It definitely represents a case of can't-see-the-forest-for-the-trees.

Rules in the business rule approach must be perceived and expressed *declaratively*, independent of processes and procedures.[3] This is the key step in moving away from "requirements" as a computer problem, and finally viewing requirements as a true *business* problem. Happily, this is also a greatly simplifying view. Suddenly, the "forest" emerges from the trees.

Understanding this fundamental aspect of the business rule approach requires careful examination of the relationship between rules and events. Intuitively, we know that rules must be enforced when certain events occur. (If nothing "happens," rules cannot be violated, and therefore they can remain dormant.) But what exactly is the connection between rules and events?

First, it is important simply to recognize that rules and events are *not* the same. This may seem obvious, but it turns out to be a common source of confusion.

> Rules and events are not the same.

To understand this, we must probe into *events* more deeply. What is an *event*? There are two ways of looking at events, both of which are correct.

---

3. We use the terms "process" and "procedure" loosely here since there are no standard industry definitions. Instead of "process," the BRS Business Rule Methodology uses the terms "task" and "action" to refer to transforms (input-transform-output). Instead of "procedure," we use the terms "workflow model" and "script" to refer to collaborations (actor-work-actor). In each case, the former BRS term refers to a business view, and the latter BRS term to a system view.

◆ From the *business* perspective, an event is when something happens that requires us to respond—even if only in a trivial way. (Usually, the response is *not* trivial.) For example, a *customer might place an order*. This is a business event that requires a well-organized response from us. Often, as discussed in Chapter 3, we try to organize our response to the event in advance—for example with a workflow model, a procedure, or a script.

◆ From an *IT* perspective, an event is when something happens that needs to be noted or recorded. This is because knowing about the event is potentially important to *other* activities, either happening during the same time frame, or that may happen in the future. In the business rule approach, of course, such "recording" is always based on pre-defined terms and facts—i.e., on the basis of some data model.

Since a data model generally presumes a *database*, the IT perspective of events often means an *update* event for data in a database.[4] In other words, an access of one of the following types will occur to a database: *create, modify* or *delete*. In fact, such an access *must* occur—or literally, the business cannot "know" about the event.[5]

The bottom line is this: In the business rule approach, a business event on the one hand, and an update (or IT) event on the other, should be viewed as mirror images of one another. One cannot happen without the other. This is illustrated in Figure 1.

Figure 1. Business Events and Update Events

Business event		Update event
Place an order	→	Create an instance of order in the database

So far nothing has been said about rules. How do such events connect with rules?

---

4. The "event" may pertain to a change of state in some object, rather than to an update to a database. For simplicity, we will use the term "update event" to loosely cover this type of event as well.

5. Except perhaps informally, based on interpersonal or intersystem "messages."

Suppose the rule given in Figure 2 has been specified for the business. The rule is given in textual form, along with the data model segment (terms and facts) to which it applies.

Figure 2. Sample Rule

> Rule: A customer must have an assigned agent, if the customer has placed an order.

First of all, note that the rule is expressed *declaratively*. This means, in part, that it does not indicate any particular procedure or process to enforce it. It is simply a rule—nothing more, and nothing less.

"Declaratively" also means that the rule makes no reference to any *event* where it potentially could be violated. The textual expression of the rule does *not* say, for example, "*When* a customer places an order, then . . . ."

This is extremely important for the following reason. "*When* a customer places an order" *is not the only event when the rule potentially could be violated*. Actually, there is *another* event when this rule could be violated. In business terms this other event might be "*When* an agent leaves our company . . . ." The corresponding update event might be "*When* an agent is deleted . . . ." This other event could pose a violation of the rule under the following circumstances:[6]

♦ The agent is currently assigned to a customer.

♦ That customer has placed at least one order.

What we find then is that the rule in question could potentially be violated during two quite distinct events. The first, "*when* a customer places an order . . .", is rather obvious. The second, "*when* an agent leaves the company . . .", might be much less so. But both are important—either will violate the rule.

This example is not atypical or unusual in any way. In fact, it is quite commonplace. In general, *all* rules (stated declaratively) produce two or

---

6. The specific update event that poses a violation of the rule is actually deletion of an instance of "is assigned to."

more update events[7] when they could be potentially violated.[8] We say the relationship of rules to events is always one-to-many.

> Every rule produces two or more update events where it could potentially be violated.

About Violations of Rules

What happens when any of the events occurs when the given rule might be violated? Several things should happen.

♦ First, no matter which event it is, at that point the rule should *fire*[9] so that the prescribed test or constraint can be applied.

♦ Second, an error message should be returned to the user (i.e., business worker) explaining why the violation occurred.

How should the error message returned to the user read? We believe the "error message" *should contain exactly the same text as was originally given for the business rule that was violated.* In the example above, this means the error message will read "A customer must have an assigned agent, if the customer has placed an order."[10]

To put this more strongly, in the business rule approach, the business rule *is* the error message. As stated earlier, we believe that information systems always should be viewed first and foremost as a *business* problem—not as a technical problem.[11] This treatment of "error messages" in the business rule approach supports that in a fundamental way.

---

7. It is tempting to say "*decompose* into two or more update events," but this is not really accurate. Rules and events are not the same thing, so the former cannot actually decompose into the latter in the strict sense of the word. Instead, we use "produce." We mean it in the sense of "can be analyzed to discover."

8. Rules do exist that are specific to an individual event, but this is the exception, rather than the general case.

9. We use the term "fire" in this book to mean loosely both "execute" (to evaluate the relevant condition(s)), *and* if necessary, "take appropriate action." Sometimes the word "fire" is used to refer to only the latter.

10. Additional text can be given to explain the relevance of the rule to the specific event, suggest corrective measures, etc.

11. In a truly *friendly* business-rule system, when a rule is violated, a procedure or script can be made available to the user to assist in taking immediate corrective action. This is discussed in Chapter 3.

> In the business rule approach, the error
> message is the business rule.

A small digression is worth making at this point. Consider the implications of this treatment of "error messages" for the front-end requirements gathering process.

In the business rule approach, the principal error messages users will see once the system is operational are the very same *requirements* they gave up-front in specifying the rules. They are literally one and the same. Well-expressed requirements mean well-expressed "error messages;" poorly-expressed requirements mean poorly-expressed "error messages." Users "get back" whatever they "put in."

This is very different from traditional approaches, where so much is often lost in the "translation" of up-front requirements into the actual running system. In the business rule approach, what you give up-front is what you will

get back later on, when the system is actually operational. This is exactly as it should be for a business-driven approach.[12] In short, the business rule approach offers practical means to close the "requirements gap" plaguing so many companies today.

---

12. The text of the actual business rule statements can be refined or supplemented, of course, during prototyping and/or system testing (or afterwards).

> The business rule approach helps to close the requirements gap.

Now let's return to the mainstream discussion. *What does the above analysis reveal about the relationship between rules and events?*

◆ First, it illustrates the basic point that rules and events, while related, are *not* the same.

◆ Second, it illustrates that there are always potentially *multiple* events where every rule could be violated. Additional examples are given in figures 3, 4 and 5 to reinforce this crucial point.

Figure 3. Sample Rule and Update Events

Rule: A customer must have an address.

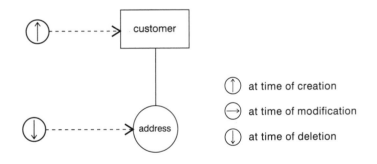

This rule produces...
    Update event #1: When an instance of customer is created.
    Update event #2: When an attempt occurs to delete (nullify) the value of address.

Figure 4. Sample Rule and Update Events

Rule: The advisor who advises a student must be a teacher
        teaching some course that student is recorded as taking.

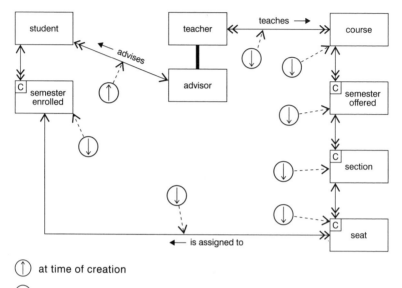

○↑ at time of creation

⊝→ at time of modification

○↓ at time of deletion

This rule produces...

Update event #1:   When an instance of advises is
                      created.

Update event #2:   When an instance of teaches is
                      deleted.

Update event #3:   When an instance of course is deleted.

Update event #4:   When an instance of semester-offered
                      is deleted.

Update event #5:   When an instance of section is deleted.

Update event #6:   When an instance of seat is deleted.

Update event #7:   When an instance of is assigned to is
                      deleted.

Update event #8:   When an instance of semester-enrolled
                      is deleted.

Figure 5. Sample Rule and Update Events

Rule: A territory must not include any non-candidate traditional gas station if it includes any ultra-service or food outlet; must not include any ultra-service if it includes any non-candidate traditional gas station or food outlet; etc.

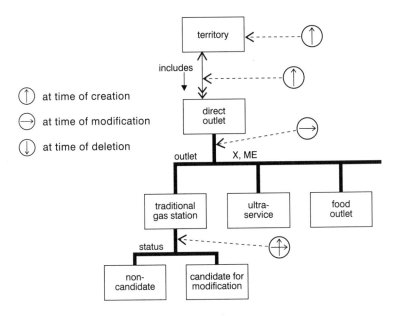

at time of creation

at time of modification

at time of deletion

This rule produces...

Update event #1: When an instance of territory is created.

Update event #2: When an instance of direct outlet is added to an existing territory.

Update event #3: When an instance of direct outlet already included in a territory changes type.

Update event #4: When an instance of traditional gas station already included in a territory adds or changes status.

The second point is perhaps the most important technical insight about rules in the business rule approach. Don't miss understanding it! The business rules approach stands traditional, procedural approaches on their heads. In the business rule approach, rules are central—*not* events.

> In the business rule approach, rules—not events—are central.

The Implications of Rules Playing the Central Role

Let's examine some of the implications of a central role for rules.

On the technical side, discovering and supporting update events becomes a crucial implementation concern. Fortunately, rule engines can often do this *automatically*—a huge boost to productivity in building reliable business software.[13]

> Automatic support for identifying and supporting update events for each rule is a key feature of rule engines.

On the business side, the emphasis on rules and their separation from events opens many new doors of opportunity. Among these opportunities are the following.

◆ *Simple consistency.* The two or more update events where a rule might be violated are likely to be embedded in at least two different procedures. (In the earlier example, this might include "Take an order" and "Drop an agent.") Often, they will be embedded in many more than that. Yet for all of the different procedures, there is only a

---

13. There are other approaches besides rule engines for supporting rules in a technical architecture. For example, update events may be detected by triggers within a server DBMS, and used to invoke user-written stored procedures automatically at the appropriate points. Another approach involves publish/subscribe facilities in object-based technologies.

single rule. That same rule
should fire when any of the
update events occurs in any
of the procedures where it
might be violated. By this
means, the business rule
approach ensures complete
consistency in the "editing
criteria" applied across all
these procedures. It also
ensures there are no "holes"
because of omissions for
less-than-obvious events.

◆ *Adaptability.* Separating the rule from the update events where it can
be violated means that the rule itself can be specified in only one
place. This means it will be easier to find—and to change quickly—
once the information system is implemented.[14] In essence, this is
achieved by *not* embedding the rule itself in the processes or
procedures where the rule might be violated.

◆ *Re-engineering.* Generally, workflows are based on responses to
events occurring in the business. Declarative rules, however—as we
have shown—are specified in *eventless* fashion. They are "pure
essence" of the business—the **Rule Book**[15] for the business "game."
This opens up almost unlimited opportunities for re-engineering the
business workflows. Indeed, the only limits will be the boundaries of
our imaginations—and common sense. *We say, rules are the key to
re-engineering workflow.*

> Rules are key to re-engineering workflow.

---

14. Or even before, if prototyping is used to allow users to "test-drive" procedures in the new
work environment.

15. A **Rule Book** is a key deliverable of the BRS Business Rule Methodology.

Rules for Control

To conclude this discussion, let's return to the question of how rules provide control in the business rule approach.

In the human body, nerves connect to muscles, the source of power for behavior. The nerves guide and control the muscles, and by that means, the resulting behavior. However, the nerves are not actually embedded within the muscles themselves.

In a business rule system, rules are like the nerves. They connect to processes—the source of power for "behavior." The rules control the processes, and by that means, the resulting behavior. However, as we have discussed, the rules should not actually be embedded within the processes.

Processes or procedures connect to rules via update events. When a process or procedure attempts to satisfy some business event, the corresponding update event will occur. This may fire one or more rules, which will determine whether the event is undertaken correctly or will produce a desired outcome. Depending on the result, appropriate action will be taken. (The exact nature of the action depends on the type of the rule. This is discussed in Chapter 5.)

Here are the essential consequences for the technical architecture of the resulting business information system.

◆ User-written "control modules" (or equivalent[16]) can often be eliminated. In other approaches, such control modules must ensure that an entire business transaction, or some stand-alone portion of it,[17] is accomplished successfully. These control modules delegate work to other process modules (e.g., subroutines), and coordinate their work. Eliminating these user-written control modules, and the whole hierarchical structure for process control, greatly simplifies overall programming.

---

16. In object orientation, this might be a control or coordinator object.

17. In DBMS terms, this might be a unit of logical work that can be committed to the database.

> ## Rules simplify programming.

◆ Control is externalized from the processes or procedures, and is established in a separate rule layer. This permits *direct* management of the rules, which in turn permits much closer tie-in to the business side. We call this *Rule Independence*[18]. This idea is a centerpiece of the business rule approach.

> ## Rule Independence is key to business-driven systems.

◆ For procedures, the result of such architecture is simplicity. To borrow a popular buzzword, taking out the rules means the processes and procedures become *thin*. This produces significant benefits in and of itself. But on a far greater scale, we believe it will revolutionize how work in the company can be organized. We examine that potential in the next chapter.

> ## Rules enable thin processes.

---

18. Refer to Appendix 1.

Chapter 3

What You Need to Know About Processes in the Business Rule Approach

In the human body, power is provided through the muscles, which enable motion. Motion results in the behavior that we see on the outside.

On the inside, however, the muscles are connected to the skeleton, which provides a framework. The muscles are also connected to the nerves, which provide control. Without these other two vital internal components, meaningful behavior would be impossible.

A business information system must have similar "power." This power—the power that produces the "motion" of the system—is provided by processes.

"Processes" are familiar to IT professionals. In general, a process takes some input—often provided by an end user working through some computer screens—and transforms it into some desired output. The process operates according to an algorithm provided by its designer or programmer. Simple as that. The only problem is that in traditional approaches, the processes are *not* all that simple. In fact, they are quite complex—and therefore quite difficult to change.

This is where the business rule approach produces the most far-reaching of its innovations. By taking the rules *out* of the processes, the business rule approach enables truly *simple* processes.

> The business rule approach enables
> simple processes.

This simplification has repercussions far beyond the limited world of IT—indeed, it has far-reaching consequences for the business as a whole. In particular, it changes the very nature of *work* in the business. We like to say, *rules revolutionize work*. This chapter suggests how that may come about.

> Rules revolutionize work.

Challenges Facing Businesses Today

Before examining how this innovation comes about in the business rule approach, let's review some of the challenges facing turn-of-the-millennium businesses, particularly as they relate to process and workflow.

Time-shock

As the rate of change accelerates, workers are constantly being thrust into new responsibilities. They must be guided through unfamiliar procedures as thoroughly and as efficiently as possible—but with minimum human intervention. The business pays a price—directly or indirectly—if their "coming up to speed" is too slow (or too painful).

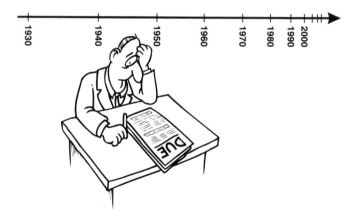

Training

The flip side of time-shock is the issue of training (aka bringing workers "up to speed"). At the risk of understatement, training is rather expensive and time-consuming. Yet as the rate of change accelerates, more and more (re)training is required.

The old cliché about phone company operators comes to mind. If telephone calls still had to be switched manually, it is said that by now everyone in the world would be a telephone operator. Fortunately, switching became automatic.

By analogy, as the rate of change accelerates, if "training" in new procedures is "manual" (requires human intervention), eventually everyone will become a trainer. Obviously, that can't happen—the "training" must be *built into* the information systems that support "doing" the procedures. We believe *business rules*—not computer assisted training, or anything like that—is how that can happen. We like to say that business rule systems are *instructional*. Later in this chapter we show how this can be achieved.

> Business rule systems are instructional.

Adaptability

In the National Football League, if a play doesn't work, it will be gone within a couple of games (possibly with a coach or two), and a new play substituted. In effect, the plays are essentially "throw-away"—"cheap" enough to discard readily, with minimum disruption or cost to the team. This is because the knowledge necessary to run the plays is embodied *elsewhere*— in the scoreboard, in the skills of the players, in the heads of the coaches— and most importantly, in the NFL rule book.[1]

---

1. A **Rule Book** for the business area is a principal deliverable of the BRS Business Rule Methodology.

Similarly, businesses need to view their own procedures as "throw-away"—that is, cheap enough to discard and replace readily when they no longer "work" (i.e., make business "yardage"). Today, this generally means throwing away whole *applications* (aka "legacy systems") and

replacing them with *new* ones, either built in-house or purchased from an outside source. This, of course, is far too expensive to do readily. So businesses are stuck with procedures that don't work well (and steadily go downhill from there)—often, watching helplessly as the competition introduces better ones.

> Throw-away procedures are a "must" to compete.

What can a business do about these challenges? We believe the business rule approach holds the answers. In the discussion that follows, we explain how business rules will fundamentally change how work is organized and managed. The implications are far-reaching—indeed we say, *rules revolutionize work*.

Putting Business Rules to Work

It is generally true that the more you know, the better you can do. If this were not the case, businesses would not spend resources on training and education—in fact, we would not spend the first decade or two of our lives in school, or bother to read, or even have libraries. There would be no dictionaries, no encyclopedias, no phone directories, or even any *Internet*.

Business rules are about "knowing"—that is, about basic operational knowledge. As we have said, business rules represent the terms, facts and rules of the business.

"Knowing" seems static (passive). So what do business rules have to do with doing work? This is no idle question—after all, it's doing the work that gets the product out the door and into the customers' hands.

A time-tested maxim in *training* is always to *build on what you know*. There are several ways in which this idea applies in developing a new approach for work (i.e., the "doing") under the business rule approach.

Actually, the maxim would be stated better as "always build on what *you know* and, beyond that, always build on what you already know *how to do.*" In the following sections, we examine each of these two points in turn.

> Always build on what you know—and already
> know how to do.

Building on What You Know

Let's spend a little time reviewing the business rule approach so we can apply its insights toward a new approach to organizing work.

Basing procedures on terms and facts

A basic principle of the business rule approach is that terms and facts (the most basic forms of "knowing") should be *shared,* and defined independently of the "doing." As discussed in Chapter 1, this is supported by developing a data model. Procedures should always comply with these pre-defined terms and facts—that is, always re-use them—instead of developing their own.[2] So the first and most basic aspect of understanding how work is organized in the business rule approach is that no procedure ever defines "data" on its own (if it intends to share it). Don't underestimate how dramatically this in itself simplifies the procedures under the business rule approach.

> Sharing common terms and facts simplifies
> procedures.

---

2. This prescription must be followed if the procedures seek to produce results to be shared by other procedures—that is, formally recorded (presumably in a database).

Rule Independence

The business rule approach really shifts into high gear, of course, by recognizing that *rules* are part of the "knowing." Like all parts of "knowing," rules should not be embedded in the "doing." We call this *Rule Independence*.

As discussed in Chapter 2, only a relatively small portion of traditional applications literally support the actual steps of a procedure (i.e., "the doing"). *Most* of the code is devoted to editing, validations, derivations, and calculations—in other words, to supporting business rules.[3] When you take the *rules* out of traditional application logic, the result is a *thin process*.

We mean "thin" in this sense: It *only* prescribes the necessary series of steps to accomplish the desired work result.[4] *Excluded* are all the rules—*and* all the "error handling" when violations of a rule occur. (We get to that crucial aspect a bit later.)

> Segregating rules produces thin processes.

Now, a picture of the new approach to "work" in the business rule approach begins to emerge. "Work" (i.e., "doing") should be viewed literally as a series of *steps* needed to accomplish a work result.[5]

A "play" in football is a good analogy. If you have ever seen a diagram of a football play in a playbook, it is literally represented as a series of orchestrated steps needed to accomplish a result (i.e., advance the ball). It is nothing more and nothing less. No rules—or penalties for violating these rules—are embedded within the play. A play simply focuses on "doing."

---

3. The code also addresses certain "housekeeping" chores (which generally also could be expressed as rules), and detection of events.

4. The word "prescribes" is important. Generally what we mean is that the series of steps "*can* be followed." This does not indicate "*must* be followed." (For example, there may be other sequences that can be followed to achieve the same results.) To say "*must* be followed" represents a rule about sequencing, and even that type rule should not be embedded in the process.

5. Often this work is undertaken in response to something a human or organization does (e.g., a customer places an order). It may also be in response to a timing criteria (e.g., time to bill customers), or some predefined condition (e.g., inventory quantity-on-hand is below a certain threshold). In the BRS Business Rule Methodology, these three types of events are called *actor*, *temporal* and *spontaneous*, respectively. Rules may be used to specify relevant conditions for the latter two types.

For business information systems, we can be a little more accurate about the "plays" the business runs. Rather than a "series of steps" to describe the "doing," we like to describe it as a "series of *requests*."

The most obvious form of these requests (usually invisible to users, of course) is a "request" to a DBMS to create, retrieve, modify, or delete *data* in a database.[6] Other types of requests may be to other *software* components, for example:

◆ GUIs or other screen objects.

◆ Service providers, such as print routines.

◆ Interfaces to legacy systems.

◆ Special-purpose rule engines.

◆ Etc.

We call a model for a series of such requests a *script*. Scripts, of course, *never* include embedded rules (or the violation-handling activity for such rules).

Examples of "canned" scripts might include the following. Note that these scripts represent *operational* bread-and-butter procedures.

◆ Take customer order.

◆ Evaluate medical claim.

◆ Book reservation.

◆ Assign professor to class.

---

6. This is how workers can share the results of procedures performed by other workers, especially when the work is not performed at the same time.

> In the business rule approach, a *script* is a
> procedure consisting of a series of requests
> with no embedded rules.

Do scripts specify requests only among software components? No! In many respects, the most important source or destination for requests in scripts is *real people*. After all, real people still do a significant amount of the work. It would be rather shortsighted to leave them out!

> Scripts involve real people too.

These people may be either *inside* the company (where they can be called *workers*)—or *outside* the company (for example, *customers*). Although all these people may be "users" of the information systems, we prefer the term *actors*. "User" suggests outside beneficiaries of information system services, whose own work and interactions are beyond our scope. "Actor" suggests someone whose own activity or role is integral to understanding and doing the work. An actor is someone whose own work is "within scope."[7]

---

7. Human actors are "within scope," but obviously outside the boundaries of the automated system.

> An actor's work is "within scope."

What can human actors do to get work done? Make requests—requests to databases, to system components, and either directly or indirectly, *to each other*.

This brings the business rule approach as applied to work into clearer focus: Human actors and software actors interacting with each other, following scripts to perform work.[8] In the thin-process, throw-away world of scripts, emphasis is on *collaboration* between actors.

> Actors follow scripts to perform work.

Implications for the Business Side

Because the scripts are "thin," the collaborations they prescribe need not be static, but rather, can be dynamic and constantly evolving. This is exactly what turn-of-the-millennium businesses need to meet the challenge of rapid change.

> The business rule approach enables adaptable, "throw-away" collaborations between people and machines.

---

8. Not all work must be scripted in advance. In fact, in a dynamic business environment, not all events and circumstances can be predicted, much less pre-scripted. This makes business information systems notably different from other kinds of computing problems such as real-time systems, process control software, system software, etc. There are several implications. First, ad hoc database access will always be a significant factor in business information systems. This is an additional reason why defining business rules directly is so important. Second, the business rule methodology should indicate when it may not be cost-effective to attempt to script work in advance, even when some event can be predicted. (This might be the case, for example, for low frequency events performed by only a few actors.) Third, the **Rule Book** can be used to guide work in a timely fashion that has not been scripted in advance, either because the event could not be predicted, or because scripting the work would not be cost-effective.

This approach is entirely consistent with current thinking about how IT should be used to transform organizational structures. Deep hierarchies, with many layers of middle management, are out. Flattened hierarchies, with empowered users and flexible patterns of collaboration, are in.[9]

More recently, a second trend has emerged that centers on automating the extended value chain, crossing organizational boundaries between suppliers, producers and customers. The real goal here is *compacting* the value chain, allowing direct, dynamic interaction between empowered actors anywhere along the way.

It is interesting to note that both the above trends involve eliminating certain types of organizational roles. In the case of re-engineering, the target is middle-layer management. In the case of compacted value chains, the target is middlemen.[10]

Both types of roles served in times past not only to filter information—the job commonly ascribed to them—but also to know and enforce business

---

9. Given these goals, we believe that functional decomposition (a technique recommended by many methodologies including traditional Martin-style information engineering) has no real value and should not be part of a business rule methodology. Functional decomposition is "wrong" in at least two respects. First, it mirrors the *form* of the old-style deep organizational chart, which is no longer appropriate. More importantly, it does not feature *collaborations* among actors—or indeed, any kind of workflow. It is outmoded, and should simply be discarded.

10. This is being called *disintermediation*.

rules. In their absence, having a **Rule Book** will become all the more urgent. Otherwise, how can the business ever communicate its rules, and ensure that the behavior of all actors remains consistent with its business objectives? [11]

> The _Rule Book_ retains knowledge
> for the business.

Back to Training

Let's now reconsider the problem of "training" in the turn-of-the-millennium business. At any given time, actors participating in scripted collaborations might be found at virtually any stage of *time-shock*. This is true no matter whether they are performing the same role for the same script, different roles within the same script, or roles in completely different scripts.

In some cases, you might find their knowledge is completely up-to-speed—but in other cases, it may seem they have suddenly dropped in from another planet. Most of the time, you will probably find them somewhere in between. This poses daunting problems not only for "training" the actors, but for building the information systems they use as well.

Application developers tend to design toward the most

---

11. As middle-level managers were eliminated in the 1980s and 1990s, essentially they took knowledge about many business rules with them. Indeed, we commonly now hear that "the systems seem to be running the business." As a result, many companies today are facing tough choices. One approach is to attempt to "mine" the business rules from the code (not an easy prospect!). The alternative is either ground-up re-engineering, or expensive (and often painful) replacements—e.g., application packages. An important lesson can be learned from this. We strongly recommend adapting a business rule approach as an adjunct to any business initiative whose direct or indirect effect could be to eliminate those human actors "in the middle." We feel this is a wise—and indeed *essential* safeguard—for the business.

advanced workers—either by necessity or by choice. This often leaves the novice hopelessly befuddled in trying to use the system. This is a long-standing problem in software development.

An alternative is building an additional stripped-down version, heavily laden with "help," for the novice worker. This alternative doubles development work, and creates new maintenance and upgrade problems. Even this solution isn't really best for all the "in-between" users—which for whatever reason, most of us usually end up being.

The solution is more or less obvious—if software were clothing, it would be called *one-size-fits-all*. The key is an environment that *stretches* as the user grows.

What this means for organizing work is that the *same* script must be usable for actors at *all* stages of time-shock.[12] This is no small challenge, but the business rule approach to organizing work provides an innovative solution.

The key lies with remembering that *all* potential "errors" (i.e., mistakes that users can make in matters related to the business) are handled by the rules, which are *separate* from the scripts. The rules, and the necessary activity to handle violations of them, are invoked (i.e., become visible to the actor) only when mistakes are actually made.[13]

The novice (i.e., time-shocked) actor will inevitably make *lots* of mistakes. To this actor the software environment will seem "big."

Actually, all the rule violation activity that makes the system seem big

---

12. The novice user, of course, benefits simply because the work is already *scripted*, providing this actor a ready-to-use template to follow. Presumably, this template is formed by those who already know what works best (aka *best practices*).

13. Users are not always required to use pre-defined scripts to do work. Instead, if sufficiently knowledgeable and properly authorized, they may elect to make requests "on the fly." Rules, and the necessary activity to handle violations of them, are invoked as always when mistakes are made.

represents in-line, automatic *training*—a business investment in getting (or keeping) that actor up to speed. We like to say that business rule systems are *instructional*.

> Business rule systems are instructional.

The advanced (i.e., up-to-speed) actor, in contrast, can be expected to make *few or no* errors. For this actor, the same software environment (i.e., script) will seem "small."

Even for the advanced actor, however, this work environment may not *stay* small all the time. This will prove especially true if the business rules themselves are in rapid flux—not unlikely for the turn-of-the-millennium business. These days, *no* worker is ever completely immune from time-shock.

> No worker is ever immune from time-shock.

The key to one-size-fits-all scripts, of course, is *Rule Independence*—that is, capturing and implementing basic business knowledge separately from the scripts. Even that, however, is not enough. Something more is necessary to guide and instruct actors effectively in doing work (i.e., in executing scripts).

In particular, the "error messages" human actors get back from the system when a rule is violated should succinctly state the *business* rule that the error represents. Only by this means can the actor get "up to speed" on the business itself.

As indicated in Chapter 2, we say therefore that in a business rule environment, the *error messages are the business rules!* In the turn-of-the-millennium business, operational workers *learn* simply by bumping up against these business rules, and by reading from the **Rule Book** in-line.

> Workers learn by reading the *Rule Book* in-line.

Building on What You Already Know How to Do

In real life, there are generally two ways in which we build on what we already know how to do. These two ways are described from the business rule perspective below. The first is relatively straightforward; the second brings business rule thinking about organizing work to its culmination.

Both of the ways for building on what we already know how to do pertain to *re-usability.* In particular, we will discuss the re-usability of scripts for doing work. Our focus will not be on software re-usability per se, but rather on the re-usability of complete *work scripts.* Think of this as *business*-level re-usability.[14]

> The business rule approach focuses on
> business-level re-usability,
> not just software re-usability.

Normal Re-use

The most obvious form of re-using "what we already know how to do" is simply embedding one procedure or script within another. The embedded procedure or script indicates how "one step" is to be taken within that larger procedure or script, whose purpose is broader or more general. Here are some simple examples from real life.

This Re-Usable procedure...	Can be re-used in...
tying your shoes	getting dressed
making spaghetti sauce	cooking an Italian dinner
driving a car	visiting your in-laws
throwing a football	running a play
typing	using a computer program

In building computer information systems, such re-use of scripts is commonplace. For example, a script for "fill out address" can be re-used in

---

14. Unfortunately, the IT trade press usually focuses on *software*-level re-usability, rather than *business*-level re-usability.

many other, broader scripts, potentially including:

- ◆ Take customer order.
- ◆ Record prospect information.
- ◆ Create shipment.
- ◆ Hire employee.
- ◆ Etc.

This form of re-use is obvious and very important. Re-use of *any* type produces consistency, which in turn, boosts productivity.

Also, the worker who already knows the embedded script will not have to learn anything new to do that part of the work. Clearly, this is highly desirable for *time-shocked* workers in the turn-of-the-millennium business.

However, such embedded ("normal") re-use involves no special use of rules. The business rule approach simply adopts it as a "given."

> Embedded or "normal" re-use of scripts
> is a "given."

Abnormal Re-use

"Abnormal re-use" is the final, crucial piece in re-thinking work for the turn-of-the-millennium business.

Abnormal re-use does *not* imply "abnormal" scripts. Rather, it implies that a script already used for "normal" circumstances also gets used under *abnormal* circumstances. Real life again provides examples.

Procedure	Normal Circumstances	Abnormal Circumstances
climb tree	recreation	escape a vicious dog
kick soccer ball	play soccer	kick penalty shot
heat item in microwave	warm-up left-overs	melt crystallized honey
make telephone call	talk to spouse	call 911 for emergency assistance
write longhand	sign check	take notes when PC is down

To understand "abnormal re-use," first it is important to understand when "abnormal circumstances" actually occur. This can be defined quite precisely for the business rule approach: *abnormal business circumstances occur when and only when a worker makes a request resulting in violation of a rule.* By implication, if no rule is violated, the circumstances are not abnormal.[15]

Another way of saying this is that *by definition*, rules define the threshold between normal and abnormal business circumstances.[16] Rules and only rules perform this role.

> Rules always define the threshold between normal and abnormal business circumstances.

In many other approaches, defining where and when abnormal circumstances occur is something of a mystery. How abnormal circumstances occur under the business rule approach, in contrast, is very well-defined. Providing for re-use of scripts for "abnormal" cases is therefore straightforward. Here is how it comes about.

1. Worker executes a script.
2. Worker makes request under that script.
3. Request produces (update) event.
4. Event fires rule.[17]
5. Rule detects violation.

What happens then is the crucial piece. One more

---

15. This does not necessarily say the circumstances are "desirable." If the request does produce undesirable results, this indicates *omission* of a rule—a different problem altogether.

16. "Threshold" implies tolerance. For a business, this generally means tolerance with respect to risk. We believe core business rules *always* ultimately address risks. Business Rule Solutions, Inc. recommends a business-oriented deliverable for establishing the business motivation for core business rules—including what risks they address—called a *Policy Charter.* Refer to "Business Knowledge—Packaged in a Policy Charter," by Gladys S.W. Lam, *DataToKnowledge Newsletter,* May/June, 1998.

17. We remind the reader that we use the term "fire" in this book to mean loosely both "execute" (to evaluate the relevant condition(s)), *and* if necessary, "take appropriate action." Sometimes the word "fire" is used to refer to only the latter.

capability is required, so that the re-use can occur.

6. When the rule detects a violation, the business rule system may have been directed (by its designers) to invoke *another* script automatically.

7. This other script presumably provides the opportunity to the original user (or possibly some other worker) to *correct* the "error" that caused the violation.

8. If accomplished successfully ...

9. This means the original work can continue under the *original* script from where it earlier left off.[18]

Here is the important point. *The script invoked by the rule under this abnormal circumstance generally should be a script also already used under normal circumstances.* This produces a form of re-usability under business rules difficult to achieve under other approaches.

> Rules enable re-use of "normal" scripts in "abnormal" circumstances.

The example below serves to illustrate. Note that this example is relatively simple. Most rules are much more complex. And keep in mind that a business area may have hundreds of such rules. Most scripts are also more complex—that is, involve a more elaborate series of requests.

Normal script	Rule	If violated, then script invoked . . .
Take customer order	601. Order must have customer.	Record customer information

Here's how this might work:

1. Order entry clerk executes "take customer order" script.

2. Order entry clerk requests creation of order without customer indicated.

3. Creation-type update event is attempted.

---

18. Note that this also is an example of an "expanding" work environment from the perception of the original worker.

4. This fires Rule #601.

5. Rule #601 detects violation.

6. Rule #601 invokes (passes control to) the "Record customer information" script.

7. Order entry uses *that* script to enter customer information.

8. This corrects the original violation.

9. Order entry clerk resumes original script ("Take customer order") from where it left off. (For example, this might permit scheduling the order's fulfillment.)

The most important observation about this example is that the script handling the *abnormal* business circumstance ("Record customer information") is presumably the script otherwise used in *normal* circumstances for that purpose.

Hopefully, that other script is already familiar to the order entry clerk. If *not*, then the episode will involve on-the-fly "training" for that time-shocked actor. What the actor actually learns is the knowledge embedded in the error message, which is simply the business rule, *Order must have customer.*

This example illustrates the full potential of business rules for re-organizing, streamlining and re-engineering "work" within the turn-of-the-millennium business. As mentioned above, a major benefit is *re-usability* at the business level, which goes well beyond simple *software* re-usability.

Additional benefits include the following:

Consistency. The script used in abnormal circumstances should be the same one used for other "normal" circumstances. This means doing the same work consistently wherever possible. Simple consistency, of course, is probably the easiest way to boost *productivity*.

Adaptability. Note that the script for the abnormal circumstance can be modified (or even replaced) *independently* of the script for abnormal business circumstances. The latter script also can change (or be replaced) independently of the former. And all *that* can occur independently of the rule—that is, be accomplished with *no* impact on the rule itself.

None of that would have been possible, of course, if the rule had been embedded within the process or procedure. So *Rule Independence* yields yet another major benefit—a new type of firewall to limit the impact of change.

> Business rules are a new fire wall to limit the impact of change.

In short, we say *rules revolutionize work*. We believe anything falling short of that will fail to achieve the full measure of adaptability that turn-of-the-millennium businesses require.

Part II

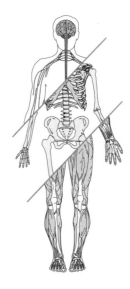

Business Rule Concepts
for the Practitioner

Chapter 4

A Closer Look at Data Models

This chapter discusses the features of data models. We start off with a quick review of the basics, in particular concerning terms and facts. Later in this chapter, we offer suggestions about generalizing the data model, in order to achieve the best results in specifying rules.

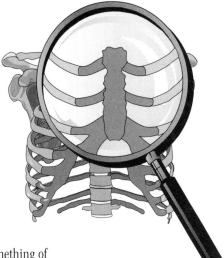

Classifying and Modeling Terms

In general, a *term* represents something of interest to the business. When a term is represented in a data model, the implication is usually that facts and rules will be defined that involve the term.[1]

Business Entities

There are several types of terms, but the most important represent *business entities*. These are terms such as *customer, prospect, shipment, order, invoice,* etc. A business entity is simply a type of person, place, thing, concept, or organization that is relevant to meeting business objectives, and that is

---

1. A term may also be viewed as something about which data will be kept. However, this discussion mainly focuses on using the data model for expressing business requirements, rather than on database design.

necessary for operating the business. A business entity is usually represented in a data model by a box. Figure 1 illustrates.

Figure 1. The employee business entity.

```
┌─────────────────┐
│                 │
│    employee     │
│                 │
└─────────────────┘
```

> A business entity is relevant to business objectives, and necessary for operating the business.

A high-level data model includes business entities and the facts that relate them. A full-scale data model may have dozens, or even hundreds of business entities. Later on, these business entities provide the basis for a database design. A closer look at business entities in database design is presented opposite.

Attributes

Other terms represent specific types of information that can be kept about business entities. These types of information are often called *attributes*. Examples include *employee-name, deliver-date-due, quantity-back-ordered*, etc.

> Attributes represent types of information that can be kept about business entities.

Different data modeling techniques portray attribute types in different ways. For the most part, these differences are purely cosmetic.[2] Figure 2 illustrates.

_____

2. NIAM and successor methodologies feature a more rigorous approach to expressing "attributes"—one that directly supports a comprehensive fact-based approach. A good reference is *Conceptual Schema and Relational Database Design* (Second Edition, 1995), by Terry Halpin, published by Prentice Hall Australia.

A Closer Look at Business Entities

Before a data model can serve as a blueprint for database design, business entities must evolve into a more precise form, sometimes called *data objects*. A data object is essentially a collection of attributes, which has direct potential for becoming a record type or table in a database design. It is assumed to possess one or more identifiers. Data objects are of three basic varieties, as described below.

Kernel type

Definition:	A data object whose instances are not naturally existence-dependent on any other(s).
Business Meaning:	Kernel types generally represent the most basic business entities in the problem domain (e.g., CUSTOMER, EMPLOYEE, etc.).
Implementation:	A kernel type usually becomes a record type or table, always with its own single, distinct identifier.

Dependent type

Definition:	A data object whose instances are naturally existence-dependent (in a direct manner) on one and only one instance of some other data object.
Business Meaning:	Dependent types generally are used to model some multi-valued aspect of another data object, especially involving structured, repetitive events or some other sequence.
Implementation:	A dependent type usually becomes a record type or table, whose two or more identifier components include the one(s) of the other data object, plus exactly one additional (usually a time stamp or sequence number).

Association type

Definition:	A data object each of whose instances is naturally existence-dependent (in a direct manner) on two or more instances of one or more other data objects.
Business Meaning:	Association types usually are used to express intersection data describing the specific relationship of instances of the "other" data object(s), rather than the instances of these "other" data objects individually.
Implementation:	An association type has the potential to become a record type or table, whose two or more identifier components include all those of the data objects related. (It should *not* add any additional identifier components.) An association also always is considered to be an implementation of a relationship, and therefore to be inseparable from it. In traditional and relational database technology, association types (or equivalent) are necessary to implement many-to-many relationships. They are optional for one-to-many and one-to-one relationships.

Figure 2. Alternative representations of an attribute.

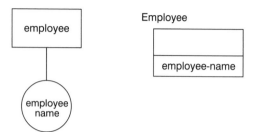

Each business entity may have several, and sometimes dozens, of attributes. Often, to avoid clutter, these attributes are not included on the data model at all, but rather are defined elsewhere.[3] A closer look at attributes in database design is presented below.[4]

A Closer Look at Attributes

Attribute

Definition: A property of a data object that is specified to represent or hold persistent values that conform to a common meaning (semantics). The values also will conform to a common representation (syntax) unless such representation is hidden (encapsulated).

Business Meaning: An attribute represents some aspect of a business entity that describes instances in a structured and predictable manner.

Implementation: An attribute usually is implemented as a field in a record type, or as a column in a table.

---

3. For example, in a CASE tool's repository.

4. Attributes in the same data model may draw upon a common set of values. For example, both *deliver-date-due* and *employee-birth-date* draw their values from *date*. A predefined set of values is often called a domain. Every domain should be given a business term as a name (e.g., *date*). Such domain names represent an additional type of term.

Other Terms

Several observations about classifying and defining terms should be made.

◆ Some terms have a plural sense—for example, merchandise, personnel, inventory, etc. If such a term has no attributes of its own, it is sometimes called an *aggregate*. An aggregate generally represents a collection of business entities. It is important not to confuse aggregates with business entities per se. A closer look at aggregates in database design is presented below.[5]

> *An aggregate is a collection of business entities, with no attributes of its own.*

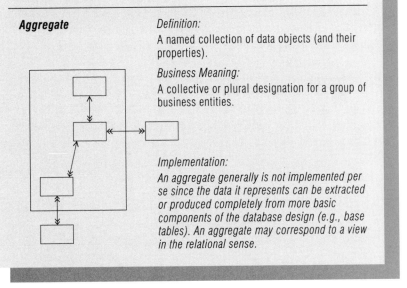

Closer Look at Aggregates

Aggregate

Definition:
A named collection of data objects (and their properties).

Business Meaning:
A collective or plural designation for a group of business entities.

Implementation:
An aggregate generally is not implemented per se since the data it represents can be extracted or produced completely from more basic components of the database design (e.g., base tables). An aggregate may correspond to a view in the relational sense.

---

5. Some business entities are associated with real-world structural composition. Examples include a case (of bottles), a deck (of cards), a car engine (with its component parts), a software package (and its component modules), etc. These are not aggregates in the sense used here. Each of these business entities may have attributes (e.g., a case may have *date-packed*). In addition, the real-world structural composition represents a fact (e.g., "case holds bottle"). Such attributes and facts are never defined for aggregates per se.

◆ Some terms may be qualified—for example, *high-risk customer*. Such a term actually denotes a subset of instances—for example, high-risk customers represent a subset of *all* customers. Such subsets are nonetheless business entities, and may have their own attributes.

◆ Some terms may refer to a collection of such subsets. For example, *gender* refers to the *male* and *female* subsets of *employee*. *Risk-class* may refer to the collection of subsets: *high-risk customer*, *medium-risk customer*, and *low-risk customer*. Such terms are treated differently by different data modeling approaches.[6]

Classifying and Modeling Facts

In Chapter 1, we indicated that every fact in a data model is always established in a sentence, which is in the form *subject-verb-object*. Such sentences fall into certain types or categories. The discussion that follows reviews three such categories.

Data modeling techniques provide specific graphic techniques for each of these categories. For the most part, differences among these graphic techniques are largely cosmetic.

Relationships

A relationship generally represents a fact involving an interaction between two (or more) business entities. A data model usually has dozens (or even hundreds) of such facts. Examples include the following.

◆ Customer *places* order.

◆ Order *is included on* shipment.

> A relationship shows an interaction between two or more business entities.

---

6. Many data modeling techniques treat such a term as a *type code*—a special type of attribute for distinguishing the "type" of instances (e.g., F=female; M=male). Other approaches consider such attributes to be a systems and/or implementation issue.

A relationship is generally represented by a line on a data model. This is illustrated in Figure 3.

Figure 3. Relationship-type Facts.

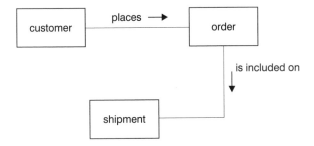

Note that each line is labeled carefully in the diagram using the appropriate verb or verb phrase. This is *essential,* since every relationship represents a fact. If a line were not labeled, its meaning would be "hidden" and thus subject to misinterpretation.

Different data modeling techniques use different conventions to represent relationship types. For example, in Figure 3, small arrows have been included so that each fact can be read correctly (e.g., "customer places order"—*not,* "order places customer").

Some data modeling techniques also recommend or require that *each* "direction" of a relationship be labeled. In essence, this recognizes that there is often more than one way to express that *same* fact, depending on one's point of view. For example, the following two sentences represent the *same* fact:

◆ Customer places order.
◆ Order is placed by customer.

Recognizing this equivalence (i.e., *unifying* these ideas as a single fact) is quite important. This equivalence might be expressed graphically as shown in Figure 4.

Figure 4. Equivalence of Facts.

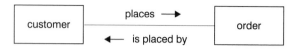

Data modeling techniques also often include some indication of *cardinality*. For each fact, this answers the question, "how many?" For example, can a given customer place *many* orders, or only a single (one) order?

Cardinality is generally expressed graphically using an appropriate terminator for the line representing a fact.[7] Sample terminations for "many" are given in Figure 5.

Figure 5. Sample terminators expressing "many" for facts.

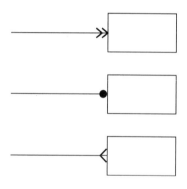

Cardinality answers the question, "how many?"

A closer look at relationships in database design is presented opposite. Although cardinality is important for database design, it is less important

---

7. Sometimes special annotation for the line is used.

for expressing facts in a high-level data model than many practitioners realize.[8, 9]

A Closer Look at Relationships

Relationship

Definition: A fact that involves two or more data objects (or a data object and itself), which can be used to record references among instances of these data objects. A relationship usually includes an indication of cardinality on both "ends," often showing a special terminator symbol. A "one" type terminator indicates that an instance of the data object on the other end may be related to zero or one instance. A "many" type terminator indicates that an instance of the data object on the other end may be related to zero, one or "many" instances (i.e., potentially more than one instance).

Business Meaning: A relationship generally reflects some interaction between the corresponding business entities. Such interaction can be described in a complete sentence, where the verb portion (never a form of "to be") reflects the relationship (e.g., "customer places order").

Implementation: A relationship generally becomes an access path in a database design, possibly supported by means of foreign keys, sets, etc.

---

8. Actually, any type of cardinality except "many" is a form of *rule*. For example, "an order may be placed by no more than one customer" is actually a rule expressed for the fact "order is placed by customer." "One" type cardinality in particular simply happens to be convenient to express directly on a data model.

9. The same is true about expressing the "optionality" of a relationship. Indicating a relationship to be *mandatory* (i.e., not optional) is a form of rule. Like cardinality, "mandatory-ness" also happens to be convenient to express directly on a data model.

ISA

A second type of fact often represented in a data model is sometimes called an *ISA*. This type of fact is so-named because the verb form "is a" is always used to form the associated sentence. The following examples illustrate.

◆ Manager *is a* employee.

◆ High-risk customer *is a* customer.

An ISA fact is unlike a relationship type, which always expresses some type of interaction (e.g., customer places order). Rather, an ISA fact expresses an underlying sameness between terms that are not quite identical. (Because they are not quite identical, the terms are *not* synonyms.)

For example, a manager is not exactly like all other employees, but is still an employee nonetheless. A high-risk customer is not exactly like every other customer, but is still a customer nonetheless.

ISA facts explicitly recognize *subsets* of business entities. For example, managers represent a subset of all employees. High-risk customers represent a subset of all customers. Such subsets are called *subtypes*. As these examples illustrate, to define such a subset or subtype, an ISA fact must reference some other set (e.g., employees or customers). This other set is called the *supertype*.

Figure 6 illustrates different ways in which subtypes can be represented in a data model. For the most part, the differences are largely cosmetic.

Figure 6. Representation of ISA facts.

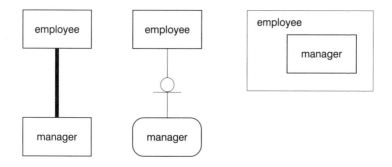

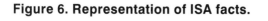
Subtypes represent subsets of business entities.

Once a subtype has been defined, it becomes its own business entity in the following sense. It may have attributes, relationships and rules[10] that do not apply to the supertype.

For example, a manager may have the attribute type *spending-limit,* and the relationship "manager manages department," which employees in general do not have. This suggests that managers are somehow "special" because they can have "more."

Indeed, another way to think about subtypes is as terms that represent special cases.[11] A manager is a special case of an employee. A high-risk customer is a special case of a customer. The focus in subtyping is always on what makes the term *different*—i.e., "special").

> A subtype is a special case of the supertype.

Looking at ISAs from the opposite point of view—that is, from the supertype's perspective—emphasizes exactly the reverse. Here the focus is on sameness or commonality.[12] For example, the business entity *employee* should be used to express what is true (i.e., attributes, relationships, rules, etc.) about *every* employee—even those who are managers.

This leads to a crucial feature of subtyping—one that greatly enhances support for the data model objective "one fact, one place" that was introduced in Chapter 1.

Consider a simple example. Every employee can have an *employee-name,* no matter whether the employee is a manager, trainee, sales representative, female, male, etc. This fact should not be expressed *individually* for each of these business entities because that would be redundant, and lead to possible

---

10. And possibly actions or operations (i.e., methods) as well.

11. Indeed, subtyping is sometimes called *specialization* for this very reason.

12. This is sometimes called *generalization*.

inconsistencies in the data. With subtyping, the fact can be expressed just once—for the supertype—and then applied to all the subtypes as needed.[13] This is called *inheritance*.[14]

> Facts in common for subtypes should be
> specified for their supertype.

Clearly, ISA facts are an important part—indeed a crucial part—of the business rule approach to data modeling. As this discussion reveals, the meaning (semantics) of ISA facts is relatively straightforward, and is closely aligned to business requirements.

Ironically, we find that technically-minded IT professionals sometimes have more difficulty with ISA facts than business professionals. This must be overcome to take full advantage of the business rule approach. Implementation of ISA facts in current DBMS technology does present certain difficulties, but generally these difficulties are not insurmountable. A closer look at ISA facts in database designs is presented opposite.

HASA

A final type of fact often represented in a data model can be called a HASA. This type of fact is so-named because the verb form "has a" can be used to form the associated sentence. The following examples illustrate.

◆ Employee has an employee-name.

◆ Order has a delivery-date-due.

◆ Line item has a quantity-back-ordered.

As these examples illustrate, a HASA fact always connects a business entity with an attribute. (This makes them unlike both relationship and ISA facts, which always connect two or more business entities.) A HASA fact indicates the business entity to which an attribute applies.

---

13. Actually, any fact defined for a supertype *must* apply to all the subtypes.

14. Inheritance opens up significant opportunities for *re-use*. This is a key feature of object orientation, which emphasizes inheritance of operations (methods). Inheritance also has important advantages with respect to business rules. First, it avoids redundant specification of attributes. In an operational database, this can avoid inconsistency in values (aka update anomalies). Second, it permits the same type of re-use for rules as OO does for operations (methods).

A Closer Look at ISA facts

ISA

Definition: A fact involving a supertype and a subtype, indicating that instances of the latter represent a subset of the instances of the former. It also indicates that the subtype inherits properties of the supertype.

Business Meaning: An ISA fact generally reflects some subsetting of a given business entity. Such subsetting can be described in a sentence using only the verb "to be" (e.g., "...is a...").

Implementation: Relational and other traditional DBMS provide no direct implementation. If not supported directly by the DBMS, three "standard" implementation alternatives are available.

1. Using separate tables. The ISA fact is implemented as a one-to-one relationship that is mandatory for instances of the subtype. This rule often may be supported using referential integrity.

2. Lumping into the supertype. The subtype is "collapsed" into the record type or table for the supertype, along with a type code whose values are used to differentiate instances. (This usually produces a significant number of nulls for sometimes-used fields, and invites misuse.)

3. Replicating into the subtypes. The attributes of the supertype are reproduced into each subtype. (This produces redundancy in the data, requiring special means to ensure consistency.)

Figure 7. Representation of HASA facts.

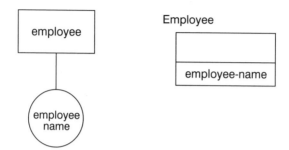

As previously discussed, HASA facts are often omitted from the graphic data model to avoid clutter. In one sense, these facts represent details that can be handled better elsewhere (e.g., in a CASE tool repository). Indeed, they may never be expressed as sentences. Still, it is important to recognize them as simply another type of fact under the business rule approach.[15]

> The logical connection of an attribute to the
> business entity it describes is also a fact.

Doing the Data Model Right for Business Rules

IT professionals with significant database experience generally agree that the hardest part of an operational database system to change or enhance is the database design itself. This will be no less true for systems following a business rule approach than for systems using more traditional techniques.

---

15. Some approaches support specifying that an attribute is *mandatory* for the given data object. This means that each instance of the data object must have a value for the attribute (i.e., that the attribute cannot be null). This is actually *rule* specified for the HASA-type fact.

> Once implemented, a database design
> is hard to change.

Change, of course, is the central fact of life for businesses today. Since businesses will sometimes have to change in fundamental ways to meet new business challenges, the potential for impact on database designs can never be eliminated completely. A good data model, however, is one that reduces to an absolute minimum the need for future changes to the database design.

How can this be accomplished? The trick is to anticipate change by generalizing the data model as much as is reasonable. The operative word is *reasonable*. "Reasonable" here means generalized without loss of meaning or clarity. It also means a reasonable chance exists that some change may actually occur in the future. If the chances of a future change are remote, then that is not reasonable.

> Database designs should be generalized to
> minimize the impact of change.

This remainder of this chapter examines several ways in which database designs can be generalized to minimize the impact of change. All these ideas depend, of course, on a solid approach to rules.

Generalizing Supertypes

As discussed above, supertypes serve several purposes in the business rule approach, as follows:

◆ They serve the objective "one fact, one place" that is so important in achieving consistency. This is achieved by placing properties common to all subtypes (i.e., attributes, relationships, rules, operations, etc.) within the supertype. This means that all rules and operations will act on them in consistent fashion.

◆ Through inheritance, they make these common properties available to all subtypes, where they can be used in specific ways appropriate in that context.

The net result of these features is a high degree of *re-usability*. When properties common to subtypes are placed in a supertype, this means they will be available to all subtypes no matter whether new subtypes are added, or existing ones are moved about (i.e., placed elsewhere in the same type hierarchy).[16] Furthermore, they will be made available in a *consistent* manner—that is, having the same meaning (semantics) as everywhere else.

The point is that by generalizing liberally, the impact of change can be reduced. Several examples illustrate.

Example 1.

Figure 8. Supertypes

lead	prospect	customer	supplier

Consider the business entities shown in Figure 8: lead, prospect, customer, and supplier. All these business entities are simply companies. The following ISA facts therefore should be recognized:

◆ Lead is a company.

◆ Prospect is a company.

◆ Customer is a company.

◆ Supplier is a company.

This implies that company is the common supertype. This might be modeled as indicated in Figure 9.[17]

Figure 9. Supertypes

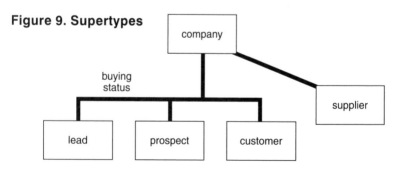

---

16. A type hierarchy is a tree-like structure of supertypes and subtypes. This "moving about" is not necessarily a disruptive database change per se, assuming the subtypes are implemented as separate tables. In this case, the change may be affected by a simple respecification of referential integrity (RI).

17. Some modeling techniques assume mutual-exclusivity across all subtypes. Since this is often inappropriate for business entities, it is not assumed here.

All common properties (attributes, relationships, rules, operations, etc.) will be associated with the supertype, *company*. That way they can be re-used (inherited) in *consistent* fashion across all the subtypes—even if new subtypes are added, or the existing ones altered.[18]

Example 2.

Figure 10. Supertypes

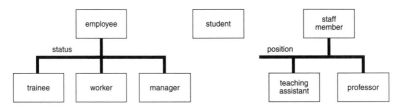

Consider the business entities indicated in Figure 10 for a university. At this university, some people are involved in more than one of these roles at the same time. In other words, the very same person could be an employee, a student, and a staff member, all at the same time. This suggests that the common properties of the business entities should be "generalized"—i.e., that a new supertype *person* can be recognized and included in the data model. This is illustrated as in Figure 11.

Figure 11. Supertypes

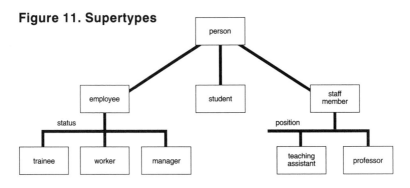

---

18. This design has an additional database advantage. Presumably, the very same company could be both a supplier and a customer at the same time. By associating common properties with the supertype, data redundancy can be avoided. For example, the company's phone number will be stored only once, rather than twice—once as a customer and once as a supplier. This avoids potential inconsistency should one or the other phone number be updated (aka update anomalies).

All common properties (attributes, relationships, rules, operations, etc.) will be associated with the new supertype, *person*. That way they can be re-used (inherited) in *consistent* fashion across all the subtypes—even if new subtypes are added, or the existing ones altered.

These examples illustrate that generalizing with supertypes provides an optimal database design in addressing certain types of change.

> Supertypes can help limit the impact of change.

Is there a danger in going *too* far with supertypes? The answer is yes—if the supertype becomes so abstract that no one can understand it, or recognize its relevance to the business. (This is *not* the case for "company" or "person," respectively, in the two examples above.) Over-abstraction occurs primarily when designers use supertypes to achieve *software* re-usability, rather than business re-usability. A consistent focus on *business rules* makes this unlikely.[19]

Generalizing Facts

An idea related to generalizing supertypes is generalizing facts. This is best illustrated by an example. ABC company expresses the following facts:

◆ Credit clerk approves order.

◆ Credit clerk is an employee.

These facts can be modeled as in Figure 12.

Figure 12. Facts

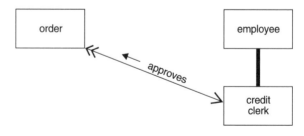

---

19. Another objection to very general supertypes is potential loss of user-friendliness. However, this can be addressed by technical means, such as relational views.

One of the aspects of businesses that change the fastest, of course, is organizational roles and responsibilities. Taking a "re-engineering" perspective on these facts, one might ask, "Why credit clerk? Is credit clerk a stable role? Why not other types of employees in the future? Why not *any* employee?"

This line of reasoning suggests that the safest alternative might be to generalize the fact "credit clerk approves order" because of the potential for change. The new version of the fact might simply be "employee approves order." The *current* responsibility (i.e., that only credit clerks approve orders) can be handled as a *rule* ("An order may be approved only by a credit clerk"). This rule potentially can be dropped or redefined in the future, as appropriate. The revised version of the data model is as in Figure 13.

Figure 13. Facts

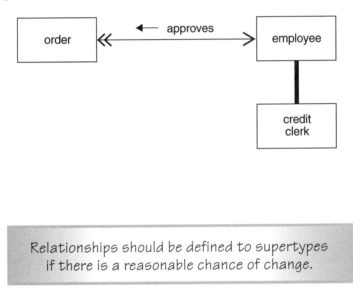

> Relationships should be defined to supertypes
> if there is a reasonable chance of change.

By generalizing the fact to the supertype *employee*, this approach permits greater flexibility to accommodate future change. This is because a change in the current rule will *not* affect the database design.

How far should facts be generalized in this fashion? As before, they should be generalized no more than is *reasonable*. Reasonable means a significant likelihood of future change.

Generalizing Cardinality

Rules provide similar types of flexibility in addressing the cardinality of relationships. The guideline here is "design for the most *general* case." The most general case is often "many" rather than "one."[20] Several examples illustrate.

Example 1.

In a petroleum company, 99% of all purchase orders are considered normal. A normal purchase order may be placed for only one well. Under exceptional circumstances (e.g., blow-outs, earthquakes, civil unrest, etc.), this rule may be violated, and a purchase order placed for multiple wells.

The most "general" cardinality for the fact "purchase order is placed for well" is "many"—even though it is a *low frequency case*. Nonetheless, the data model should address the more general "many" case, as Figure 14 illustrates.

Figure 14. Cardinality

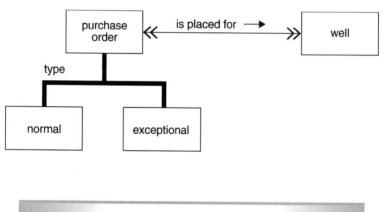

> "Many" type cardinality is safer if there is a reasonable chance of change.

In this model, the cardinality of the relationship "is placed for" is indicated as "many" into well because this is the most general case. A rule is

---

20. In relational terms, using an association type, rather than a foreign key—even if a relationship is currently "one"—is the safe bet.

expressed that applies only to the normal case, limiting the cardinality to "one." Note that this rule is easily dropped (or altered) in the future, should a change in business policy make its current specification inappropriate.

Example 2.

Company XYZ currently permits an order to be shipped to only a single destination. However, customers are beginning to request multi-destination orders, so this requirement may have to be addressed in the future. The most "general" cardinality for the fact "order is shipped to destination" is "many"—even though this is not the current business policy. The data model should address this more general "many" case, in anticipation of future change.

Figure 15. Cardinality

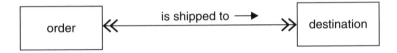

Figure 15 illustrates. In this model, the cardinality of the relationship "is shipped to" is indicated as "many" into destination because this is the most general case. A rule ("An order may be shipped to at most one destination") is expressed that establishes the *current* business policy, which limits the cardinality to "one." Note that this rule is easily dropped (or altered) in the future, should the possible change in business policy actually occur.

By generalizing cardinality, database designers can achieve maximum flexibility for future change. This is because a change in the current rule will *not* affect the database design.

How far should cardinalities be generalized in this fashion? As before, they should be generalized no more than is *reasonable*. Reasonable means significant likelihood of future change.

Generalizing Time

In expressing facts and cardinality, it is easy to overlook the time dimension—i.e., past and future—and simply express "right-now" versions. These give *point-in-time* views.[21]

Here are some examples of point-in-time views of facts and cardinality.

◆ An employee may be assigned to at most one department.

◆ A railroad car may arrive in at most one station.

As these examples suggest, the point-in-time view often reflects a "one" type cardinality.

Clearly, the point-in-time view is very limited. *Over time*, the cardinality is clearly *not* "one," but rather "many." The *points-over-time* view of the facts and cardinalities might be as follows.

◆ Over time, an employee may be assigned to many departments.

◆ Over time, a railroad car may arrive at many stations.

These revisions clearly suggest a "many" cardinality.

Unfortunately, the actual facts are a bit more complicated. (This is not unusual in addressing time, which is always the hardest part of a data model to do well.) In particular, the following observations are true:

◆ Over time, an employee may be assigned to the *same* department more than one time.

◆ Over time, a railroad car may arrive at the *same* station more than one time.

The key to addressing the complexity of these relationships is to realize that actual *events* are occurring in the business. These events can be named—producing new terms. The new terms are as follows.

◆ The *assignment* of employees to departments.

◆ The *arrival* of railroad cars at stations.

As represented in the data model, it is important to recognize that these events are *not* either of the following:

◆ *System* events (i.e., system activity per se).

◆ *Update* events (i.e., database activity per se).

---

21. The point-in-time view is often used intentionally to simplify requirements in producing first-cut or high-level data models. This can be quite helpful in getting started.

Rather they are a reflection of true business events that occur in a predictable, repetitive, structured manner.

Generalizing time in a data model means including business entities to represent such events directly.[22] The data models in Figure 16 illustrate.

Figure 16. Time

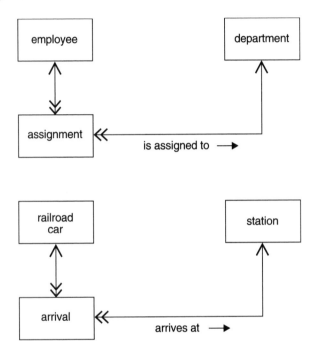

Generalizing the original facts by including event-type business entities achieves the following:

◆ It permits the true points-over-time relationships to be expressed. For example, it permits two or more assignments of an employee over

---

22. These business entities are usually *dependent entity types*. Such dependent entity types can be viewed as recording changes of state in some *other* business entity (e.g., employee or railroad car). Business problems require full accommodation of the time dimension (i.e., of history and future). This, incidentally, is one of the characteristics that makes business problems distinct from other types of problems (e.g., real-time systems, process control, system software, etc.).

time to be to the same department. (Note that each assignment, however, is to only one department.)

> A points-over-time data model limits the impact of change.

◆ It permits other rules to be expressed directly. For example, for railroad cars, such a rule might be the following: "Successive arrivals of a car may not be at the same station." Note that many such rules may change over time. By generalizing time in the fashion described above, such change can be accommodated with minimum impact on the database design.[23]

> A points-over-time data model better supports rules.

---

23. As always, of course, the chance of such change should be a *reasonable* one.

Chapter 5

A Closer Look at Rules

In this chapter, we discuss the basic varieties of rules, and examine related questions. The objective is a deeper understanding of rules on their own terms. This is important since rules are an independent component in the business rule approach.

Ways in Which Rules Can Exercise Control

Rules come in two basic varieties with respect to the type of action they take: *rejectors* and *projectors*. These varieties are discussed individually below.[1]

Rejectors

Many rules are naturally *rejectors*—that is, left to their own devices,[2] they

---

1. This discussion is based on *The Business Rule Book*, Second Edition (1997), published by Business Rule Solutions, Inc.

2. Often, such rules are *not* merely left entirely to "their own devices." For example, as discussed in Chapter 3, when a rule fires and a violation is detected, a user-friendly rule system might automatically offer a script for the user to follow in correcting the violation.

simply *reject* any update event[3] that would cause a violation to occur. The specific sequence of activity would occur more or less as follows.

1. A user initiates a procedure to do some work—for example, "Take a customer order."

2. The user requests an update event to record the results of the work—for example, "Create an instance of order in the database."

3. The update event causes a rule to fire[4]—for example, "Order must have a ship-to address."[5]

4. The rule checks whether the user has actually included a ship-to address in the order. Suppose the user has *not* done so.

5. The rule causes the update event to be *rejected*—that is, the transaction fails, and the order is *not* created in the database.[6]

This analysis reveals the following important point about *rejectors*. In their native form, you might say that rejectors are very narrow-minded. Either the user plays by the rules, or the work will not be accepted.

REJECTOR

---

3. As in Chapter 2, the term "update event" generally presumes an *update* event for data in a database. In other words, an access will occur to a database of one of the following types: *create, modify* or *delete*. However, the "event" may pertain to a change of state in some object, rather than to an update to a database. For simplicity, we will use the term "update event" to loosely cover this type of event as well.

4. As in Chapter 2, we use the term "fire" in this book to mean loosely both "execute" (to evaluate the relevant condition(s)), *and* if necessary, "take appropriate action." Sometimes the word "fire" is used to refer to only the latter.

5. For simplicity, we ignore whether this rule fires immediately, or is deferred until the end of the transaction or unit of work (i.e., until the actual time of "commit.").

6. For simplicity, we ignore the opportunity to invoke an appropriate procedure (i.e., script) to allow the user to correct the violation immediately, and then continue the original work. Such capability was discussed in Chapter 3.

In other words, *rejectors* are intently focused on work being done correctly.[7] If there is any question about the quality of the work—that is, the quality of the *data* that would result from it—the work simply will be rejected (until correct). In other words, rejector-type rules *insist* upon data quality, and they do so by active, real-time intervention in on-going work.[8]

> Rejector-type rules address data quality.

This brings us to another point. The business rule approach emphasizes real-time enforcement of rules at the *operational* level of business activities. The objective is to coordinate *on-going* activities, to ensure optimal (i.e., correct) results on an as-you-go basis in doing work. This frequently involves rejector-type rules. This is a different emphasis than in historical use of expert systems, as discussed later.

> The business rule approach emphasizes operational-level, in-line enforcement of rules.

Projectors

A projector-type rule is the exact opposite of a rejector-type rule in a fundamental way. Specifically, a projector-type rule never rejects update events. Instead, it always accepts them—and automatically takes some *other* action as a result.

---

7. In database technology, correctness is called *integrity*.

8. In Chapter 2, we emphasized that the *definition* of rules should be data-based (i.e., based on the terms and facts included in a data model). Here we see how the *operation* of rules can also be data-based. In general, a rule cannot directly prevent a user from doing something "wrong" inside a process. A process is more or less like a black box whose semantics are unknown. However, the rule *can* prevent the results of the process from being recorded. It does this by rejecting the *data* that the procedure "wants" to "leave behind" once it finishes executing (or commits a transaction) if the process does not follow the rule.

In general, a projector can be expressed as *"if this, then that too."* In other words, a projector literally *projects* "this" to "that." [9]

Projectors seem much "friendlier" than rejectors. This is because they do not inhibit update events, but rather provide additional "mileage" for them. [10] Projectors fall into three categories as given in the box below. A simple example is given for each category.

Categories of Projector-Type Rules

Enablers	Copiers	Executives
This category of rule may be used for inference.	This category of rule may be used for setting values.	This category of rule may be used for executing processes.
Example: A person should automatically be considered a woman, if the person is a female and is over twenty-one.	*Example:* The total fee a student owes for a semester must be set to the base tuition for that semester when the student registers for that semester.	*Example:* *Calculate-order-total* must be executed for an order when the order is closed.

In summary, projector-type rules provide automatic value-added behavior. They can be used for a variety of purposes, including the following.

◆ To eliminate "given" behavior as a user responsibility, providing

---

9. The projection from "this" to "that" may or may not be immediate when the event occurs. This depends on the particular rule engine, and on how it is used. In classic use of expert systems, for example, the "firing" of rules was often delayed—i.e., not in-line with actual on-going events. More recent practice, however, has emphasized firing rules on a more immediate, in-line basis. In general, this proves much more effective.

10. This is not entirely accurate. For example, a projector can be used to switch on (i.e., enable) a rejector-type rule in appropriate circumstances. The net result would be potential rejection of update events in those circumstances.

automated assistance in performing operational work.

◆ To derive or infer new potential knowledge from an existing set of facts, providing automated assistance in making decisions.

> Projector-type rules provide automatic value-added behavior.

Projectors extend the overall range of rules significantly. The complete spectrum of rules is examined more closely in the box below.

The Spectrum of Rules

The business rule approach covers the entire spectrum of rules, from the simplest type of constraints, to advanced forms of inference. The goal is a unified approach to the capture and management of all such rules. We believe this is the key step in moving toward the goal of true *knowledge management.*

To illustrate the extremes in this spectrum of rules, consider the following analogy.

A Baseball Situation

Suppose it is the bottom of the seventh inning, with 2 outs, 2 strikes on the batter, and 2 base-runners. The score is tied. The batter is left-handed.

Inference-type rules might . . .

. . . help choose the best relief pitcher under these circumstances.

A constraint-type rule might . . .

. . . ensure that the batter still gets only 3 strikes even if the pitcher is changed.

About Suggestions

As discussed earlier in this book, the business rule approach emphasizes rules as a principal means to exercise *control*. This chapter has discussed several ways in which this occurs.

Rejectors exercise control by preventing certain update events from being successful (i.e., by rejecting updates).

Projectors can exercise control by removing responsibility for certain "given" behaviors from users, and ensuring that such behavior *always* occurs under appropriate circumstances.

In the business rule approach, rules also can be used to *influence* behavior, rather than to control it directly. In such case, a rule can be viewed as a guideline or heuristic (i.e., as a *suggestor*[11]), rather than a hard-and-fast rule. An example illustrates.

Consider the following rule:

> **Rule #116.** A customer *must* have an assigned agent, if the customer has placed an order.

Let's make a simple change in the wording, switching "must" to "should."

> **Rule #116 (Revised).** A customer *should* have an assigned agent, if the customer has placed an order.

Now, the original rule has been converted from a constraint into a *suggestor*. The following points about this transformation should be noted.

---

11. From *The Business Rule Book,* Second Edition.

Form

The form of the suggestor remains exactly the same as before. The *only* change is that the word *"must"* has been changed to the word "should."

This represents an important aspect of the business rule approach—one that should be reflected directly in languages for expressing rules. Put simply, if you have a language for expressing constraints for behavior, then you already have a language for expressing *guidelines* for behavior. This unification is an important feature of the business rule approach. It also shows how the business rule approach has significant potential to play a fundamental role in knowledge management.

> Suggestors are expressed in the same form as other rules.

Firing

The firing of the suggestor remains exactly as before. Specifically, a suggestor fires when any of the two or more update events occurs where it could be "violated."

The suggestor is not the same as these events, however—and should never be embedded in the procedures that address the events. This allows for easy change in the suggestor. Such adaptability always results from *Rule Independence*.

> Suggestors fire the same way as other rules.

Enforcement

The enforcement level of the suggestor is the *only* thing different from before.

As a constraint, a rule will take whatever action is necessary for enforcement. For Rule #116, this presumably means *rejecting* any update event that might violate the rule. As a suggestor, no such enforcement action is taken. The update event is *not* prevented. Instead, the user will merely be informed of the guideline.

A suggestor is merely a rule that fires, but is not currently enforced.

As always, the rule text should pop up on the user's screen. For the suggestor, however, the text is *not* an "error message," but rather a guideline. It *informs* the worker that under the given circumstance, some particular type of action (update event) is, or is *not*, appropriate. In other words, suggestors impart business knowledge in such a way to influence how work is conducted—but do not attempt to control the work outright.

A suggestor imparts business knowledge to influence *how work is conducted.*

About Exceptions

When introduced to the business rule approach, the first reaction some people have is that their business has far more exceptions to rules than rules per se. They question how all these exceptions can be handled in any organized fashion. This is a valid concern.

The business rule approach offers no silver bullet to the *business* problem of "too many exceptions to rules." It does, however, offer a very simple *technical* answer. This technical answer, in turn, does have implications for business process re-engineering and streamlining business operations. We will comment briefly on that momentarily.

First, let's examine the question of exceptions to rules from the technical point of view. Consider the following example.

> **Rule #135.** A library card may be held by at most one borrower, *unless one of the borrowers is Bill Gates*.

This rule includes a clear-cut exception. The normal rule is "A library card may be held by at most one borrower." The exception is, "don't enforce this rule if Bill Gates is one of the borrowers for the library card."

Careful examination of this exception reveals something quite interesting. This can be seen more clearly if the statement of the exception is reversed, as follows.

> **Revised version #1:** If Bill Gates is one of the borrowers for the library card, then don't enforce the rule.

Now replace "don't enforce" with "automatically disable." The exception now reads as follows.

> **Revised version #2:** If Bill Gates is one of the borrowers for the library card, then *automatically disable* the rule.

If you follow this sleight-of-hand closely, what emerges is . . . *another rule!*

Specifically, what emerges is a *projector-type* rule. This new rule does the following. It watches for events that could affect evaluation of the condition "if Bill Gates is one of the borrowers for a library card."

If the condition is found to be true, the new rule takes an action automatically in response. The particular action it takes is to disable (switch off) the original rule, so that it will no longer be enforced for that particular library card.

The bottom line: *The exception to the rule is simply another rule!*

As a technical matter, the business rule approach *always* views exceptions to rules as simply more rules. This puts exceptions to rules on the same playing field as all other rules.

> In the business rule approach, exceptions to rules always represent more rules.

This is important for another reason—one that touches on methodology, on business process re-engineering, and indeed, on the business itself. Briefly, the reason is simply this—the business rule approach recognizes that *all* rules cost something.

> All rules cost something.

The cost of rules is not simply the direct cost of implementation and maintenance of systems. It also lies in the "hidden" costs associated with documentation, training, administration, and *time*. In a time-shocked business, of course, time may be the most precious commodity of all. Your business doesn't need *more* rules—it needs fewer (*good*) rules!

> Fewer *good* rules is better.

Firing Sequence

Since events play such a central role in organizing rules, it seems fitting to return to events in concluding this chapter.

In Chapter 2, we pointed out that a crucial insight of the business rule approach is that every rule produces two or more update events where it could be potentially violated. This idea is central to *Rule Independence* and to all the benefits it offers.

It turns out, however, that the *reverse* is also true: Every update event can cause *more* than one rule to fire.

Consider the update event "Create an instance of *order*." This update event can potentially fire many rules, including those listed below.

Rule #4902. An order must have a fulfillment expediter.

Rule #31. An order must indicate the customer that placed it.

Rule #116. A customer must have an assigned agent, if the customer has placed an order.

Rule #68. A customer's credit rating must be good, if a customer has placed an order.

This raises the following crucial technical question: *In what sequence should these rules fire?*

A first point to remember about the business rule approach is that many rules are *rejectors*, as opposed to projectors. In fact, all four of the rules above are rejectors.

When an update event occurs, *all* the rejectors that fire as a result must be satisfied. If *any one* is not, the update event will be rejected. In that sense, it doesn't matter too much in which sequence the rejectors fire.[12]

For projectors, the sequence of firing can make significant difference in the "final" state a transaction achieves.[13,14]

What position does the business rule approach take on the technical issue of firing sequence? This is a complicated issue, but the short answer is this. *Explicit control for firing sequence (like exceptions to rules) simply requires more rules.*[15]

> Explicit control for firing sequence requires
> more rules.

Events and Business Rule Methodology

The final step in understanding the relationship between rules and events is a subtle one, but one that developers cannot afford to ignore. Indeed, it is central to choosing an appropriate *methodology* to develop business rule systems.

Let's review the points we've made about the relationship between rules and events, and then examine the implications. In doing this, remember that the workflow, procedures, and/or scripts that users follow in doing work are generally organized on the basis of *events*. As discussed in Chapter 3, rules

---

12. From a user-friendliness and/or workflow perspective, however, the sequence of firing even for rejectors can make a difference in certain cases.

13. This is why the sequence of firing has always been a central concern in expert systems, which are projector-oriented.

14. The sequence of firing among rejectors and projectors can also make a significant difference. For example, the firing of a projector-type rule might "fill in" a value that would then satisfy a rejector-type rule. Firing the rejector-type rule first might produce an unwarranted violation.

15. A good rule engine offers many "default" firing sequences that minimize or eliminate this issue as a developer's concern. Beyond that, using such rule engines in a prototyping mode can allow users to "test drive" the rules. This approach can be used to discover sequencing preferences.

external to these scripts provide control.[16]

As we have noted, the relationship of rules and events is as follows.

◆ Every rule produces two or more update events when it could be violated.

◆ Every update event can fire more than one rule.

The implication is that a rather complex weave of rules, events and scripts will result. In particular, we will find the following.

---

16. For convenience, we use the term *script* for any detailed procedure workers can follow. Scripts are discussed in Chapter 3. In object orientation, a script might be called a *use case*.

◆ A rule is likely to be fired in unexpected scripts, which are specified (and executed) by workers not directly associated with specifying the rule.

◆ A script is likely to fire unexpected rules, which are specified by workers not directly involved in specifying (or executing) the script.

Does this weave of potentially "unexpected" encounters with rules complicate matters? The answer, of course, is *no*. A business information system is no more entangled by having independent rules than is a game of chess, or baseball, or football by following a **Rule Book**. In a very real sense, a business *is* a set of rules. We believe the value of *Rule Independence*[17] speaks for itself.

Rather, the point we take from this is that your business rule methodology must put business rules on at least an equal footing with workflow models and/or scripts.[18] Basing your methodology purely on workflow models and/or scripts[19] simply produces the raw power to do work—muscles for the business to flex. A **Rule Book** represents a well-developed nervous system. Without it, there is no guarantee your business will ever use its muscles to work *smart*.

---

17. Refer to Appendix 1.

18. This is a key feature of the BRS Business Rule Methodology.

19. Including "use cases."

Appendix

The Declaration of Rule Independence

Twenty-Nine Principles for the Business Rule Revolution

by Ronald G. Ross

1. Rules are rules are rules.

2. Rules are not process, not procedure, not data, and not objects. They should not be embedded in any of these.

3. Rules imply constraints on processes.

4. Rules cannot constrain processes directly, only the results they seek to leave behind. Rules always constrain data that persists in some fashion.

5. Rules can be applied to any data that persists in any fashion. Data may persist during a session about the execution state of processes; rules therefore can be applied to workflow, as well as to databases.

6. Rules must be explicit. No constraint ever is assumed on any persistent data unless a rule has been specified explicitly.

7. *Rules govern sequence. Assume no constraints on concurrency, serialization or sequencing among executions or states unless rules are specified explicitly.*

8. *Rules govern selection. Assume no constraints on which instances of appropriate types can be involved in operations unless rules are specified explicitly.*

9. *Rules govern derivation. Automatic calculation should be based on rules.*

10. *Rules govern lots of other things, including counts, co-existence, relative position, successions, comparisons, freezes, copying, timing, synchronization, and so on.*

11. *Rules can be classified according to what they evaluate. This classification should be independent of any other specification component, including processes and data.*

12. *Rules should be expressed declaratively, in natural-language sentences, each of which includes a subject and a predicate. If it cannot be expressed, then it is not a rule.*

13. *Rules should be modeled declaratively. Rules are based on truth value; the algorithm used to evaluate this truth value is hidden.*

14. *Rules normalize. Truth values are data, and can be normalized like any other data.*

Appendix

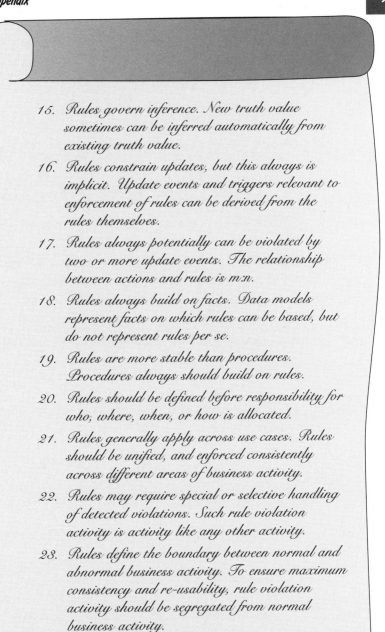

15. Rules govern inference. New truth value sometimes can be inferred automatically from existing truth value.

16. Rules constrain updates, but this always is implicit. Update events and triggers relevant to enforcement of rules can be derived from the rules themselves.

17. Rules always potentially can be violated by two or more update events. The relationship between actions and rules is m:n.

18. Rules always build on facts. Data models represent facts on which rules can be based, but do not represent rules per se.

19. Rules are more stable than procedures. Procedures always should build on rules.

20. Rules should be defined before responsibility for who, where, when, or how is allocated.

21. Rules generally apply across use cases. Rules should be unified, and enforced consistently across different areas of business activity.

22. Rules may require special or selective handling of detected violations. Such rule violation activity is activity like any other activity.

23. Rules define the boundary between normal and abnormal business activity. To ensure maximum consistency and re-usability, rule violation activity should be segregated from normal business activity.

24. *Rules include all exceptions to rules. Exceptions to rules are rules.*

25. *Rules, including exceptions to rules, always cost something. "More rules" is not better.*

26. *Rules are basic to what the business knows about itself—that is, to basic business knowledge. Rules need to be nurtured and protected.*

27. *Rules require management.*

28. *Rules, in the long run, are more important to the business than hardware/software platforms.*

29. *Rules, and the capacity to change them effectively, are key to improving business adaptability.*

Originally appeared in "The Declaration of Rule Independence" by Ronald G. Ross, *DataToKnowledge Newsletter* (formerly *Data Base Newsletter*), Nov./Dec., 1995, p 24.